Off-the-shelf
assemblies

Off-the-shelf
assemblies

101 acts of worship for
secondary schools

W. E. Beales

First published in 2002 by
KEVIN MAYHEW LTD
Buxhall, Stowmarket, Suffolk IP14 3BW
E-mail: info@kevinmayhewltd.com

9 8 7 6 5 4 3 2 1 0

ISBN 1 84003 850 0
Catalogue No 1500476

Cover design by Angela Selfe
Edited and typeset by Elisabeth Bates
Printed in Great Britain

Contents

Foreword

Many of us involved in politics try and grapple with the consequences of human failure and selfishness. We know that if we are to build a better world, it must start with me, and it must start with a change of heart. I have only ever met one person who has changed my heart, and that is Jesus Christ.

But it is no exaggeration to say that the majority of children growing up in Britain today have never heard about him. How could they? Few of them go to church or Sunday school, the television rarely presents a positive message based on scripture, and in very few homes is the true nature of the gospel ever discussed. About 8 per cent of the British people regularly attend a place of worship, leaving quite a few who never hear about the things he did and said.

The greatest challenge facing the Church today is not the knowledge that the vast majority of our fellow citizens have considered the gospel, found it wanting and rejected it – they haven't. The reality is that most people have not even considered the meaning of life, where they have come from and where they are going. They have never given God more than a passing thought.

None of us wants to live in a country where the gospel message is rammed down our throat or where there is pressure to embrace certain beliefs. The greatest gift that God has given us after life itself is the freedom to choose. But if the next generation of our citizens is to have the ability to choose to follow Jesus they have to hear about him in the first place.

What better place than the school assembly? This collection of off-the-shelf assemblies is a very welcome step in helping to make sure that all of our children have the opportunity to think about the origins and destiny of life, and consider for themselves whether they wish to pursue an exciting walk of faith.

But the message has to be attractive, not dry and boring. What I particularly like about this collection is the rich varitey of ideas of how to present profound but thought-provoking truths to all age groups. Each of these ideas is attention-grabbing. I would be surprised if some of these assemblies did not make the most unlikely listener stop and think.

The first assembly is called 'A step of faith'. This is the starting place for all of us. The final offering is headed 'You can make a difference'. This neatly sums up the power of the book. Hearing about Jesus will cause many young people to take those first steps of faith. We know from history and our own experience that this will change their lives, and more than that: help to make a positive difference to the lives of others and to our country.

This book is an important new resource. I pray that it will be used with much fruit all over the United Kingdom.

GARY STREETER MP

Introduction

Collective acts of worship offer pupils and staff the opportunity to explore and share beliefs; consider the importance of prayer, meditation and silence, the relevance of ideas and beliefs to their own lives; to think about the needs of others and to develop a sense of belonging to a community. It offers the opportunity to reaffirm, interpret and put into practice the values and ethos of a school.

The main aim of the collective act of worship is to search for the meaning and purpose of life.

Assemblies can and do play an integral part in the spiritual, moral and cultural development of young people in our schools. Observations by OFSTED inspectors and advisers suggest that whilst the latter two aspects are adequately developed through school assemblies and curriculum initiatives, the spiritual dimension is often underdeveloped.

The purpose of this collection of assemblies is to provide material for secondary school assemblies that addresses the spiritual perspective within a Christian context and linked to the central teachings in the Bible.

They are designed to raise those important questions that all of us, at some point, try to find answers to. Each assembly has been used in an 11-18 secondary school, where the format has been a hymn (related to the theme of the assembly), the delivery of the short talk by the head teacher and finishing with a personalised prayer.

They do not represent the complete range of assemblies given to the pupils but complement other types of assembly given by pupils and staff.

It is hoped that the material will be a useful resource for ideas that could either be used in their present format or developed into longer assemblies. Alternatively, they could be focal points for discussion in PSHE or religious studies lessons.

The aims of the material are:

- to provide all pupils with knowledge and insight into Christian beliefs and values and to create opportunities for religious experience in a way which develops their self-knowledge and spiritual awareness;

- to enable pupils to make moral decisions through application of reason by establishing a framework of values which regulate personal behaviour through principles rather than through fear of punishment or reward;

- to teach the principles which separate right from wrong;

- to encourage pupils to relate effectively to others, take responsibility, participate fully in the community and develop an understanding of citizenship;*

- to know the rights and responsibilities of individuals within a social setting;

- to enable pupils to reflect on how the values and beliefs of people impinge on all aspects of their lives.

*Citizenship becomes part of the national curriculum from 2002 and a number of the assemblies naturally lend themselves for inclusion in the broader discussions related to citizenship. These are listed below and include the relevant page reference.

Human Rights – 13, 15, 19, 29, 33, 37, 41, 79, 81, 101, 109, 114, 118, 126, 131, 137, 141, 157, 180.

Democracy and autocracy – 15, 29, 33, 41, 54, 81, 118, 126, 131, 145, 157, 180.

Community involvement – 37, 45, 54, 66, 74, 101, 118, 122, 126, 137, 139, 155, 180.

The legal system – 23, 37, 45, 54, 109, 114, 126, 129, 131, 146, 180, 189.

Global citizenship – 19, 35, 59, 66, 109, 139, 180, 183.

Money and finance – 21, 23, 34, 59, 66, 74, 79, 81, 83, 95, 101, 114, 145, 146, 155.

Co-operation, conflict and tolerance – 15, 23, 33, 37, 41, 109, 118, 126, 141, 157, 180, 189.

Sustainable development – 23, 68, 79, 139, 183.

Central and local government – 15, 29, 33, 45, 81, 109, 126, 137, 146, 161.

The media in society – 19, 21, 29, 66, 74, 79, 95, 101, 103, 114, 118, 149, 155, 176.

Hymn references
The Source and *The Source 2*, Kevin Mayhew Publishers
Songs of Fellowship, Kingsway Music, 1993

W. E. BEALES, 2001

A step of faith

Talk

One of the great joys of parenthood is in watching the development of your child as they grow. This is especially true in the first eighteen months of life where a baby learns very rapidly and acquires the skills of crawling, eating, smiling and talking. But perhaps the greatest moment is when they take their first steps, and learn to walk. Babies are very trusting and have complete faith in their parents and it is through placing their trust in them that they are able to take those first faltering steps.

Some people see becoming a Christian as a blind leap of faith, the type of faith needed by the baby in taking their first step. However, this view completely ignores the wealth of historical evidence, the prophetic writings, the multitude of personal testimonies and the signs and wonders all relating to the life, death and resurrection of Jesus Christ.

Indeed, the real step of faith for all Christians is in believing not that Christ died, but that he came back to life – that he had conquered death. Without this step of faith the last two thousand years of Christian worship has been futile. However, millions of Christians throughout the world will testify that, in taking this step of faith they have found the meaning of their life on earth and a sure hope of the life that is to come in heaven.

If there is no resurrection of the dead, then not even Christ has been raised. And if Christ has not been raised, our preaching is useless and so is your faith. 1 Corinthians 15:13-14

In accepting the truth of the resurrection of Jesus Christ it gives us the confidence to face any trials and difficulties in our daily lives because we are secure in the knowledge that there are greater things awaiting us beyond our earthly life.

The Bible tells us that Christ was born to die and through his death we have been forgiven our wrongdoings and promised everlasting life provided we put our trust in him.

Are you willing to secure your future by taking this step of faith?

Prayer

Father, we thank you for sending your only Son, Jesus Christ, to save us all by dying on the cross and for the hope of eternal life through his resurrection.

Hymn   We believe in God the Father
The Source, 541; *Songs of Fellowship*, 572

All things bright and beautiful

'All things bright and beautiful' is a well-known hymn of praise. It praises God for the wonders of creation.

It is very easy to accept the beauty of nature around us, not noticing the shapes, shades, colours and smells of everyday objects. We often take ordinary things for granted.

Take an orange, a common enough object in every supermarket. I suppose we might describe it as round and orange in colour. Suppose, however, that you had been deprived of access to sound and sights, locked away from the real world for many months; how would you view it then?

Brian Keenan was kidnapped in Beirut in 1985 and was held captive for four and a half years in a 6 foot long and 4 foot wide cell. Then one day his eyes are almost burned by what he sees – the sight of an ordinary fruit fills him with an overwhelming sense of wonder and awe.

He was so in awe of the orange that he felt unable to eat it, for fear of destroying its beauty and form. He was fascinated by its shape and texture, the richness of its colour, and sat in absolute wonder that such an insignificant fruit could fill him with such completeness and love.

Brian noticed every single detail. The colour was so wonderful he could not destroy it by eating the orange.

The Bible tells us that since the creation of the world God's invisible qualities, his eternal power and divine nature, have been clearly seen, being understood from what has been made, so that men are without excuse and know of his presence. Even though surrounded by the wonders of creation, the familiar backdrop to our lives, we often overlook the fact that they demonstrate the mystery and power of the omnipotent God.

Do you not know? Have you not heard? The Lord is the everlasting God, the Creator of the ends of the earth. He will not grow tired or weary, and his understanding no one can fathom. Isaiah 40:28

Have you become blind to the world around you?

We acknowledge you, Father God, as the creator of the infinite range of plant and animal life on earth. Help us to keep our eyes, ears, hearts and minds attuned to the wonders of your creation and be thankful for this fingerprint of your awesome power and the love you show for each and every one of us.

Hymn   All things bright and beautiful
The Source, 14; *Songs of Fellowship*, 14

Ambition

During our school years we tend to have a number of ambitions, whether they are playing for Manchester United, being a famous inventor, becoming Prime Minister or doing great things for humanity. Upon reflection, these might not seem particularly realistic ambitions; they are daydreams, which fluctuate according to who or what is dominating the headlines of the day.

Many would agree that as they gain more of life's experiences and an awareness of their strengths and weaknesses, their ambitions become more realistic. It is no detrimental thing to have ambitions; they help sharpen practice and give a clear purpose and direction for the work that you do. In school, pupils who succeed are generally those who have clear ambitions for the future – whether in the academic, sporting, musical or social domain.

At the outset of one's working life, it is sensible to think through the various career routes and establish a vision of where you want to go. Someone starting out as a trainee chef may have an ambition of owning their own restaurant; a junior doctor may have the ambition of becoming a consultant in a leading teaching hospital; or an amateur cricketer may have the ambition of playing for their county and country.

Whilst ambitions can give a purpose to our work, we need to be wary of the underlying reasons for our ambitions. In the Bible we are told the story of the tower of Babel. The people had the ambition of building the tallest building in the world. There was no purpose in this building other than to satisfy the selfish motive of making a name for themselves. The story in Genesis goes on to describe how God thwarted this self-centred ambition by making it impossible for the peoples to communicate with each other.

The ambition of Hitler was to conquer the world but his motives were evil and corrupt and it was inevitable that he would fail. In James' Gospel we are also warned of the dangers of having wrong motives for our ambitions.

Who is wise and understanding among you? Let him show it by his good life, by deeds done in the humility that comes from wisdom. But if you harbour bitter envy and selfish ambition in your hearts, do not boast about it or deny the truth. Such 'wisdom' does not come from heaven but is earthly, unspiritual, of the devil. For where you have envy and selfish ambition, there you find disorder and every evil practice. James 3:12-14

Prayer

Lord, help us guard against selfish, self-centred ambition and corrupt practices. Assist us in making effective use of the talents you have so freely given so that we can use them in service to others and as a witness to your generosity and love.

Hymn

Set my spirit free that I might worship thee
Songs of Fellowship, 494

Anchor of hope

Talk

The anchor on a boat serves a number of functions.

Firstly, it prevents the boat from drifting on the tide. This stops it going in or out with the tide. Secondly, it can be used to protect the boat when there is a strong wind against it. The idea is that the anchor can hold the boat so that it faces into the wind and prevents it from keeling over. And lastly in a storm. In this case, the anchor is put out and trails behind the boat to prevent it from turning side on. It is not much good if the wind is coming from behind the boat – hence the expression 'riding out the storm'.

Throughout life we will be faced with a variety of challenges and, rather like the boat, we need to have a firm anchorage to prevent us drifting with the tide or sinking in a storm. Drifting on the tide is almost imperceptible. One moment everything is secure and safe, the next moment we have drifted far from where we were.

Temptations come our way and we begin to bend the rules to justify the actions that we take. We move slowly away from right living. Individually each small drift is insignificant, but collectively it has an enormous impact on our lives. The temptations may be things of the world, perhaps friends or family; we need a strong anchor to resist the pressure to confirm and compromise our standards.

Storms are those moments in our life when the unexpected, and often tragic, events happen. The loss of a loved one, losing a job, failing an examination, financial ruin and so on. Without a firm anchor and hope for the future we are often unable to ride the storm – we become depressed, angry, jealous, resentful, hurtful and revengeful. These severe storms come into every life. They are circumstances beyond our control, real crisis, disasters or life-threatening situations. Tough times never last, but tough people do.

Whilst the boat has an anchor, we have God. Our hope is anchored in God, because through him we can ride the storms of life, the unexpected gusts, the changing wind direction and the ebb and flow of life. As David writes:

I am confident of this: I will see the goodness of the Lord in the land of the living. Wait for the Lord: be strong and take heart and wait for the Lord. Psalm 27:13-14

We all need hope when the situation appears hopeless. When we face the storms of life we need faith and patience because these will enable us to endure and place our hope in God as our anchor for life.

Prayer   Father, lighten our darkness, protect us from danger and give us peace
               at times of trial in our journey through life.

Hymn   God of all comfort
               The Source, 129; *Songs of Fellowship*, 136

Armchair critics

The media coined the phrase 'couch potatoes' to describe the sedentary lifestyle of the vast majority of the population. By this, they meant we had become a nation of television watchers, content to watch the action from the comfort of our armchairs without having to participate in the range of events and activities on show. We had become a nation of bystanders.

In a similar vein, it is possible to argue that we have also become a nation of armchair critics. It is extremely easy to criticise from the comfort of our home the events that we read of in the newspapers and watch on the television. How easy it is to see the mistakes that the footballer made, or to ridicule the apparent lack of knowledge of a participant on *Who wants to be a millionaire?* We are in danger of losing sight of reality as we habitually make critical judgements and criticisms from a distance.

We watch the nightly news and view without apparent concern the atrocities that occur daily throughout the so-called civilised world. In being armchair critics, we have become immune to the plight of real people in the real world. We are cocooned in our self-righteousness and our own security that blurs the distinction between fictional violence in films and actual violence portrayed on the news and in documentaries.

Christians face a particular challenge because there is no such thing as an 'armchair Christian'. They have been commissioned by God to respond to the injustices that pervade our society; they have to enter the real world and challenge those things that they know are wrong. This is not an easy thing to do and can lead to difficulties, frustrations and challenges to one's life, but it can never be convenient to be a Christian choosing when or when not to act.

I recently read the account of a young man who had been held in solitary confinement in a Burmese prison for standing up for what was right despite the cost to his personal freedom and safety. In his account he describes some of the conditions he endured during his imprisonment.

His beatings followed a regular pattern. On each occasion, 15 men trooped into his cell armed with 3ft wooden clubs, wound around with rubber strips to ensure that the deep bruises did not show up until two weeks later.

The punishment went on for three days. On the first day, only one of them laid into him, savagely administering a couple of dozen blows. The second day, the squad arrived at 1.30 pm; they roughed him up, ripping his shirt and poking him with their clubs.

He received two black eyes, a broken nose, lumps on his head and bruised cheeks. He prayed, saying that he would do whatever was required as he finally came to his limit of endurance.

God had protected him for a year and he had to trust that something would turn up.

A few days later he was released – God had answered his prayer. His crime – standing up for democracy and freedom of speech against a corrupt government that did not recognise Christian precepts.

It is not always convenient or popular to be a Christian in our world and we cannot be silent and ashamed about Christ's words. There is no such thing as an armchair Christian.

Prayer

We beg you, Lord,
    to help and defend us.
Deliver the oppressed,
    pity the insignificant,
    raise the fallen,
    show yourself to the needy,
    heal the sick,
    bring back your people
    who have gone astray,
    feed the hungry,
    lift up the weak,
    take off the prisoner's chains.
May every nation come to know
    that you are God,
    that Jesus Christ is your Child,
    that we are your people,
    the sheep of your pasture.
Clement of Rome (c. AD 200)

Hymn

Fight the good fight with all thy might
Songs of Fellowship, 107

Beauty is only skin deep

Over the past twenty years, there has been an exponential growth in the range of treatments and products for beauty care. These range from anti-wrinkle creams to muscle toning equipment and health farms. Where once only the few could afford the luxury of masseurs and the occasional weekend at a health farm, it has now become common practice for many more to make use of the facilities and products on the market.

Despite the claims of the promoters of the various treatments and beauty products the truth of the matter is that people still age and die. There is nothing wrong with the ageing process although more and more people seem to hanker for solutions that keep them young, fresh and vibrant, much as they remembered it in their youth. Perhaps there is nothing wrong in wanting to keep one's looks, or in wanting the sustainability of youth when you are in your late fifties or early sixties. However, we need to question our priorities – is it that important to have an outward appearance that tries to mask the truth that the inner self has indeed aged?

Have we become so concerned with outward appearance that we are no longer concerned with the inner-self? Are we more concerned with making impressions through visual indicators than by the way we relate with each other and the values that underpin the nature of our character?

Jesus was never very much concerned with a person's outward appearance, but was always concerned with their inner feelings, the values and beliefs that drove them. An outwardly attractive individual doesn't necessarily make an inwardly attractive person if what drives them is self-centred greed and egotism. Jesus warns us not to be deceived by outward appearances but to concentrate on actions which let us know what motivates the person, for that will tell us more about their true character than the outward appearance does. In talking about the teachers of law at the time, Jesus said the following:

You clean the outside of the cup and dish, but inside they are full of greed and self-indulgence.
You are like whitewashed tombs, which look beautiful on the outside but on the inside are full of dead men's bones and everything unclean. In the same way, on the outside you appear to people as righteous but on the inside you are full of hypocrisy and wickedness. Matthew 23:25, 27-28

Living our Christianity merely as a show for others is like applying beauty treatments on the outside only. When we are pure on the inside our outward appearance of beauty and cleanliness won't be a sham, and our actions will reflect both the inner and outer quality of our life and the beliefs that drive us.

Prayer

Keep our bodies fit, keep our minds keen, keep our thoughts pure, keep our words clean and wholesome for the sake of Jesus Christ our Saviour.

Hymn

Here I am, wholly available
The Source, 161; *Songs of Fellowship*, 167

Bad news — good news

Talk

It is not surprising that on reading through newspapers we are left with the impression that the world seems to have lost its way and has become a place where evil seems to triumph over good. For example, one weekend's editions contained reports on *(replace with topical reports as appropriate)*:

- the 100ft submarine being built by drugs barons to illegally import cocaine to the United States;

- pet food being sold in Britain to top restaurants as quality meat in a multi-million-pound fraud;

- two sisters receiving jail sentences for robbing and beating to death an 87-year-old pensioner who had, over the years, befriended them, often helping them out and providing them with money when they were in need;

- another £40 million given to the millennium dome project on top of the £600 million it had already received;

- the discovery of a very large hole in the ozone layer over Antarctica.

With so much evil to be found in the world it is hardly surprising that people can become downcast and hold a pessimistic view of the future. Some may even be prompted to ask, 'What hope is there for those who seek to do what is right and abide by the law?'

King David, the second king of Israel, an ancestor of Jesus, wrote in around 1000 BC about similar problems and used powerful words of encouragement in his psalms to show how, by placing our complete trust and faith in God, justice would prevail and the good and righteous would be rewarded with eternal life.

Here are some of the words from Psalm 37 in which David invites us to trust in the Lord and wait patiently for him to act.

Do not fret because of evil men
or be envious of those who do wrong;
for like the grass they will soon wither,
like green plants they will soon die away.

Trust in the Lord and do good;
dwell in the land and enjoy safe pasture.
Delight yourself in the Lord
and he will give you the desires of your heart. . . .

Refrain from anger and turn from wrath;
do not fret – it leads only to evil.
For evil men will be cut off,
but those who hope in the Lord will inherit the land.

A little while, and the wicked will be no more;
though you look for them, they will not be found.
But the meek will inherit the land
and enjoy great peace. . . .

The salvation of the righteous comes from the Lord;
he is their stronghold in time of trouble.
The Lord helps them and delivers them;
he delivers them from the wicked and saves them,
because they take refuge in him.
Psalm 37:1-4, 8-11, 39-40

We should never envy evil people, even though some may be extremely popular or excessively rich and successful. No matter how much they have, it will fade and vanish like grass that withers and dies.

Those who follow God live differently from the wicked and, in the end, will have greater treasures in heaven. What the unbeliever gets may last their lifetime, alternatively it may not. What you get from following God lasts for ever.

Prayer

O Lord our God,
    who has called us to serve you,
    in the midst of the world's affairs,
    when we stumble, hold us;
    when we fall, lift us up;
    when we are hard pressed with evil, deliver us;
    when we turn from what is good, turn us back;
    and bring us at last to your glory.
Alcuin (c. AD 735-804)

Hymn

Fear not, rejoice and be glad, the Lord hath done a great thing
Songs of Fellowship, 106

Being a Christian can be tough

Talk

Are they servants of Christ? . . . I am more. I have worked much harder, been in prison more frequently, been flogged more severely, and been exposed to death again and again.
2 Corinthians 11:23

Even if I should choose to boast, I would not be a fool, because I would be speaking the truth. But I refrain, so no one will think more of me than is warranted by what I do or say.
2 Corinthians 12:6

This account was written nearly two thousand years ago by Paul the Apostle. It details some of the trials he had faced as he spread the word of the Gospel through the Roman Empire. It is interesting to note that only a few years previously he himself had persecuted and been responsible for the deaths of a number of Christians. This stopped when Christ entered his life and transformed him when he became a Christian. Although later executed by the Romans, his faith and trust in Christ never faltered.

We are unlikely to have our faith in Christ tested in quite the same way; none the less, being a Christian can still be tough and challenging. Every day there will be opportunities for the Christian to show their commitment to Christ by their actions. For example:

- in the home by helping to wash up when you would prefer to be watching television;

- at school by helping others, being polite and courteous and being honest about why the homework hasn't been completed;

- by having the courage to speak out when you see wrong being done to others;

- by challenging bullies;

- by giving your time for the service of others;

- by donating some of your spending money to charity;

- by not fighting with your brothers and sisters;

- by not always taking that last piece of cake;

- by not sulking when you don't get your own way;

- by admitting you were wrong;

- by always telling the truth, however hard this is and the pain it may give you and others;

- by telling others of your faith and sharing your experience of Christ with them;

- by reading your Bible and praying to God for guidance, help and forgiveness for the wrongs you have done.

Remember, actions speak louder than words and the Christian's faith will be judged by their actions. As James, Jesus' brother, said:

What good is it, my brothers, if a man claims to have faith but has no deeds?

You see that his faith and his actions were working together, and his faith was made complete by what he did. James 2:14, 22

Let us also take heed of what God said through the apostle Paul when he wrote his letter to the Ephesian church:

For it is by grace you have saved, through faith – and this not of yourselves, it is the gift of God – not by works, so that no one can boast. Thus, just as a professed faith in Jesus Christ without good works is dead, so good works without God-given faith in Jesus Christ is dead. Ephesians 2:8-9

Prayer

Father, help us in our daily lives to be good examples of the trust we place in you. Guide us in our thoughts, words and deeds. Help us to refrain from doing those things that we know are wrong, and the courage to stand by what is right.

Hymn

The Lord's my Shepherd, I'll not want
The Source, 486; *Songs of Fellowship*, 537

Being qualified

Talk

One of the main purposes of schooling is to provide young adults with the necessary qualifications to enter the job market, so that they are employable. A scan through the job adverts in newspapers shows that employers usually give an indication of the type of person they are seeking and the qualifications they will need to have.

Most require you to have at least grade C in English and Maths at GCSE together with three or four other subjects. For professional jobs, such as accountancy, teaching, doctors, etc., A-levels together with a university degree are the norm. Of course, it doesn't follow that having the qualifications means you will be able to do the job. The ability to work in a team, honesty and integrity, punctuality, reliability, initiative and drive are additional important qualities.

I have yet to see in the job vacancies an advert for being a Christian, even though, unlike other jobs, becoming a Christian is open to every-one. There are no formal qualifications, no interviews and limited financial and promotion prospects – so what are the entry criteria?

1. The first step is to accept that you are not perfect, admit that in your life you have thought, said and done what is wrong, and be willing to correct every thought, word, action and habit which you know to be wrong.

2. The second is to believe in Jesus Christ and the fact that he died on the cross to forgive us the wrongs we have committed in God's sight.

3. The third is to allow Jesus Christ to control the way you live. This means every part of your life – your work, your friendships, your time, your money – all must come under his control.

There are no exams or interviews but by following these three simple conditions, you will not only guarantee an occupation for life but also life everlasting.

Why not put your application in today, you are guaranteed to be shortlisted and offered the post!

Prayer

Lord Jesus Christ, we know we have sinned against you in our thoughts, words and deeds. We have not done so many good things. Forgive us, and help us to place our trust in you as our friend and saviour.

Hymn

Abba, Father, let me be yours and yours alone
The Source, 1; *Songs of Fellowship*, 1

Big Brother is watching

Talk

In his famous novel, *1984*, George Orwell describes the life of Winston in a totalitarian state, where every word and action is monitored and recorded. The state scrutinises every facet of the individual's life through two-way tele-screens that can both transmit and receive information. Everyone is under the watchful eye of Big Brother as they go about their daily routines. Through this monitoring, the state is able to exercise complete control over people's lives.

This is not the same as the television programme of the same name. In the first series of *Big Brother*, you may have witnessed nasty Nick and his underhand methods, the flirtatious Melanie and the removal each week of one of the contestants. *Big Brother* attracted a viewing audience of millions and those with the internet were able to visit the *Big Brother* website to observe the daily lives of the participants in the programme. It was great entertainment and the audience were given some degree of control and power by being able to vote out members of the group on a weekly basis.

How natural was the behaviour of Nick, Claire, Craig, Melanie and the other participants knowing that everything they did was being recorded and observed? How well did we know the contestants? Although we could listen to their words and see their actions, how well did we know what made them tick, their value systems and their beliefs? How real were their lives in the virtual reality of the stage? I wonder how our behaviour would change or be modified if we thought Big Brother was watching us 24 hours a day.

Christians believe that there is a Big Brother watching us in our daily lives and, unlike the cameras in the programme, can probe our inner thoughts and feelings going beyond the purely physical imagery as seen in the television programme. This Big Brother, unlike the audiences who could only vote for the removal of a person from the programme, has the power of life and death. God is not only our judge but the jury as well.

Throughout the duration of the series, all of the contestants of *Big Brother* were able to remain within the bounds of the strict rules and regulations the programme laid down as a precondition for their entry to the show. However, the same cannot be said with regard to our keeping all of God's Law as laid down in the Old Testament, indeed the Bible tells us that all have sinned and fallen short of the glory of God. Even though this is sadly true and will exclude many from being admitted into heaven, God, because of his great love for the world, has provided a way for us to be right with him and thus receive eternal life.

As you go about your daily work, remember that there is an unseen, all pervasive Big Brother watching you all the time.

This righteousness from God comes through faith in Jesus Christ to all who believe. Romans 3:22

Prayer

You have taught us to do unto others as we would have them do to us; grant that we may be considerate in our judgements, gracious in our speech and charitable in all that we do. Guide us when we are in doubt or perplexed and, as we strive to be just and true, so may we constantly seek to order our lives in accordance with your will.

Hymn

Teach me to live, day by day, in your presence, Lord
Mission Praise, 627
Teach me to dance
The Source, 469

Bridge over troubled water

Talk

Bridges are fascinating engineering structures designed to join one place with another. We often hear the phrase 'to bridge the gap' a clear analogy with the purpose of the physical structure. A more common phrase that has recently been introduced to the language is 'to build bridges' in relation to forging links between people or organisations. It can also refer to the repair of damaged personal relationships between individuals or groups.

Central to successful bridge building is the need for firm foundations on either side of the bridge. If either foundation is weak, the whole structure will collapse. The bridge structure is also designed so that the forces of compression and tension in it are shared out equally between the individual members that comprise the bridge. This makes the bridge much stronger and less likely to collapse when placed under excessive stress and strain. Furthermore, the bridge is designed to allow the two-way flow of traffic thereby maintaining communications between both ends.

Similarly, we can view our relationship with God as being like a bridge. For a sound relationship, the bridging mechanism needs to be without structural defects and the foundations on which it is built firm and secure. There also has to be two-way traffic across the bridge to ensure that it can respond rapidly to changing circumstances and for keeping dialogue between the two sides open.

We can build a firm foundation by reading the word of God as recorded in the Bible by God's messengers over thousands of years. We can communicate through prayer from one side of the bridge to the other through the supportive span of Jesus Christ. Messages from the other side can be received through the work of the Holy Spirit, and by sharing our load with other Christian members we are all able to take the strain at times of increased stress and pressure and keep the bridge intact.

In the early seventies Simon and Garfunkel recorded a hit single whose title best illustrates the purpose of the bridge between ourselves and God: it was called 'Bridge over troubled waters'. The purpose of the link with God through Jesus Christ is to guide us from our earthbound foundation to the foundation in heaven. It is not an easy journey, and the foundations may have to be built many times before they can support the load, but once in place, it provides a quick and accessible route to the One who created us all.

How far are you in constructing your bridge with God?

Prayer

Father, help and direct us. Hold our hand when we are at risk of failing. Through your Holy Spirit, enable us to construct a bridge built on firm foundations so that access to your heavenly kingdom remains open at the end of our life on earth.

Hymn

Faithful One, so unchanging
The Source, 89; *Songs of Fellowship*, 89

Chameleon behaviour

Talk

Chameleon is the common name for any lizard well known for their ability to change colour when frightened, in response to light, temperature or any other environmental changes. Using this ability, they are able to blend into the background, often avoiding dangerous situations.

We can all be a bit chameleon in our behaviour. For example, how often have you found yourselves agreeing with your friends when in reality you totally disagree with them? How often have you been economical with the truth in order to keep the peace and not stand out as someone different?

True, it is sometimes wiser to blend into the background than stand out from it, but this is not always the case. For example, if you see someone being bullied and you say nothing you would be demonstrating a capacity for cowardice rather than wisdom. It is often fear of becoming the victim that prevents us from standing out from the crowd to defend the principles of right and wrong. Becoming chameleon in our behaviour is an easy way out of difficult situations, but it is not necessarily justifiable.

Being a Christian is not always easy, particularly in countries where oppression, discrimination, violence and intimidation are the normal ways of suppressing those who stand out from the crowd.

Even in this country, those who profess to believe in Christ can experience ridicule and pressure to conform. This is especially true for young Christians who are struggling for independence on the one hand and acceptance by friends on the other. There is considerable pressure on them to adopt chameleon-like behaviour, by denying they are Christians and their faith in God.

Nothing is new about this. Throughout history, Christians have experienced hardship, torture and death for standing by what they believe, rather than blending into the background like a chameleon.

The question you must ask yourself if you are a Christian is this: are you willing to stand by what is right or are you developing chameleon characteristics which prevent your true identity and faith being known?

Prayer

Through Jesus Christ, bestow us with the courage to stand by your principles and not to be afraid of witnessing our faith in you with those whom we meet. Help us to stand out from the crowd as people steadfast in our faith.

Hymn

Fear not, for I am with you
Songs of Fellowship, 105

Christmas card fever

Talk

A few weeks ago, I received my first Christmas card of the season. It was from a former colleague in Kent to whom I have not spoken since 1979 when I left the area. It bears a picture of a reindeer clad in festive boxer shorts with the handwritten message, 'Have a great one!' Love Tom and Claire. [Adapt to your own situation.]

The fact is that Tom and Claire cannot know for sure that I am still breathing let alone in a position to have 'a great one'. Year after year, their greetings fall faithfully through the letterbox, posted first class. I am on their mailing list and that is that. By receiving their greeting, I am participating in a ritual which is redundant for me but reassuring for them. They have entered the 'Christmas spirit'. They have done their bit.

In most cases nowadays, of course, the giving and receiving of Christmas cards has become little more than a habit, a reflex action as insincere and automatic as the 'have a nice day' you get from the average McDonalds assistant. With Christianity all but sidelined in our pursuit of more important matters, such as acquiring Play Station 2, cards are as likely to be used as vehicles for our personal vanity as messages of peace and goodwill.

Professor Adrian Furnham of University College London, who has written a paper on card psychology, believes the sending of Christmas cards is an obsession with its own rules, eccentrics and natural order. The sending of cards with snow-scapes and wintry scenes is a sign of an inspirational person, joke cards are sent by the socially unskilled while charity cards indicate the more serious-minded person attempting to escape some of the commercialism of Christmas.

Whatever the reason for sending Christmas cards we all need to remember what it is that we are celebrating. The exchanging of gifts and cards pales into insignificance when compared to the gift God gave mankind two thousand years ago. For through the gift of Jesus Christ our lives can be transformed. Through this gift we have been promised forgiveness of our sins and eternal life; having faith in him is the only condition and faith is something that is available to all, irrespective of our social and economic standing. A free gift to any who wish to take advantage of it – have you responded to this gift yet?

Prayer

To the King of ages, immortal, invisible, the only God, be honour and glory for ever and ever.

Hymn

Thou didst leave thy throne and thy kingly crown
The Source 2, 1015; *Songs of Fellowship*, 555

Communications satellite

On 3 November 1957, Laika, a black and white dog, was sent into orbit round the earth in *Sputnik II*. She was the first living being to leave earth and make a flight into space, and on 12 April 1961 the soviet test pilot, Yuri Gagarin, was the first human being sent into orbit round the earth, in *Vostok 1*. The entire flight lasted for only 108 minutes.

Since the early days of space flight, men have landed on the moon, space probes have been sent to Venus and the outer planets. No doubt, it is only a matter of time before humans will be able to participate in journeys lasting many years as they travel to distant planets and galaxies.

The world of communication is dependent on the use of satellite technology. Communications satellites are placed in geostationary orbit, 36,000 km above the earth's surface, and used to bounce radio signals around the globe, so that 24-hour communication between any two places on the earth's surface is possible. It has enabled those in America to watch the English cup final live, and similarly those in this country to follow events in America as they happen. The technological advances in communications satellites has, indeed, made the world a much smaller place.

An active satellite is the generic name given to the type of satellite that acts on the signal it receives, before transmitting it back down to the receiving station on the earth's surface. The other type of satellite is known as a passive satellite, which merely receives signals from one place on the earth and reflects them to another, without acting on them, or changing them in any way.

God is, in many ways, like our geostationary communications satellite acting on the signals we send him. Of course, we don't use radio waves for this, but communicate through prayer. However, our receiving antenna are not always quite tuned in to receive his communications, and it is only through meditation, study of his word, practice and the Holy Spirit working in us, that we can begin to receive and decode the information he is transmitting. Unlike the passive satellite, which only deflects incoming signals, God's antenna detects, decodes, interprets and answers our prayer signals before redirecting them to tuned receivers back on earth. And, like a geostationary satellite, it makes no difference where you are on the earth's surface, communication is always possible and available 24 hours a day.

Know that the Lord has set apart the godly for himself;
the Lord will hear when I call to him. Psalm 4:3

And will not God bring about justice for his chosen ones, who cry out to him day and night? Luke 18:7

Prayer

God grant us the serenity
    to accept the things we cannot change,
    the courage to change the things we can,
    and the wisdom to know the difference.
Reinbold Niebuhr (1892-1971)

Hymn

Lead us, heavenly Father, lead us
The Source, 311; *Songs of Fellowship,* 321

Dear Christians

Talk

Family, friends and colleagues in the workplace can present particular challenges for the Christian. For example, suppose one of your work colleagues is misusing company time, or one of your family is a bit too liberal with members of the opposite sex. Suppose you have a friend who betrays a confidence, or you discover they are working, whilst at the same time claiming benefits from the state. I am sure we can all think of instances where our Christian principles could be compromised by the people we associate with.

The dilemma, for the Christian, is what to do in these circumstances. Are you going to be direct, approach the situation, and challenge the behaviour you know is offensive in God's sight, or ignore it? Challenging the problem head-on could lead to broken relationships, divided families and bullying in the workplace; ignoring the problem makes a mockery of your Christian principles. And therein is a real danger, since if your Christian faith is well known, what message is being given about your faith to others, especially if you apply elastic principles according to the circumstances you face.

Not only is their behaviour challenging, it is also challenging your faith.

There can be no compromise, since Christians have been commissioned by Christ to be witnesses to their faith, upholding the principles of right and wrong and the precepts that underpin God's work in the world. We can pray about the situation, we can pray for courage, and we can pray that others acknowledge their sins. However, we cannot pray that the situation goes away, since the trials it brings are a test of your faith and whether your faith is evidenced by your actions. Perhaps Paul gives us the greatest example of how we should act.

Even though, as a Roman citizen, it would have been relatively easy to renounce his faith and enjoy the trappings of life as a Roman citizen, Paul determinedly stood by his faith despite the difficulties he experienced as a result. He did this without complaining, and in full knowledge of the likely outcomes for him personally. His strength came from his unwavering trust in Christ, who had transformed him from a persecutor of, to a soldier for, Christ.

Indeed, such was his faith that he welcomed the challenges, assaults, brutality, imprisonment and removal of privileges as a test of his faith. And through them he grew in spiritual maturity and closeness to Christ who gave him the strength and courage to handle any situation, and through his writings became one of the greatest witnesses to Christ we have. Had he not challenged the challenging behaviour, we might never have had Paul's letters and the remarkable testimony they contain to guide and strengthen us in our faith today.

By challenging the challenging behaviour, you too are witnessing for Christ.

How have you responded to Christ's invitation to go and make disciples?

Then the eleven disciples went to Galilee, to the mountain where Jesus had told them to go. When they saw him, they worshipped him; but some doubted. Then Jesus came to them and said, 'All authority in heaven and on earth has been given me. Therefore go and make disciples of all nations, baptising them in the name of the Father and of the Son and of the Holy Spirit, and teaching them to obey everything I have commanded you. And surely I am with you always, to the very end of the age.'
Matthew 28:16-20

Prayer

Lord, open our hearts and minds to your words so that we become willing disciples in helping others to find salvation and everlasting life through you.

Hymn

O Jesus, I have promised
The Source, 391; *Songs of Fellowship*, 418

Deep rooted

I have a gardening implement called a 'daisy rooter' and, as the name implies, it is used for uprooting daisies. It consists of a long handle, with two prongs attached to the end of it. The idea is to hook the prongs under the daisy, and use the long handle to lever the root out of the ground. The roots to a daisy can be quite long, and are generally held firmly in the ground; the deeper they go, the more difficult to extract. More often than not, the root stem snaps leaving a remnant below ground; whilst the flower and rest of the root are removed. The effect of this is that over a period of a few days, the remnant begins to sprout new foliage, and a new daisy plant emerges. The only sure way of removing the weed is to carefully dig the whole of the plant and root out of the ground. Even then you have to watch for the tell-tale signs, that other plants are not shooting up as the daisy propagates itself. It is best to tackle daisy roots with the 'daisy rooter' early in spring, when the ground is still soft following the winter rains, and the roots have not had time to develop a strong hold in the ground.

There is an analogy between extracting the root of a daisy from the ground and sin from our life. God gave humans free will, and the misuse of free will leads to temptation and sinful behaviour. Take, for example, betting. One could argue that on the surface it is a relatively harmless activity. However, the driving force for gambling is money – why else bother wagering a bet? The difficulty comes when a succession of successful bets leads to an obsession with gambling. We are probably all familiar with families that have been destroyed by the gambling addiction of a member of the family. Before long, devious ways are found to service the increasing stranglehold of gambling on the victim, so that the sins of stealing, lying and cheating become firmly embedded within their character. Like the daisy root that has been allowed to grow too long, it is difficult to extract the sinful nature from the addicted gambler.

There are many other examples where sinful nature has been allowed to nurture and grow within the person; like the daisy, postponing its extraction from our lives makes it increasingly difficult to remove. Then there is the danger that although people claim to have controlled a particular problem (selfishness, drink, drugs, stealing, etc.), the urge isn't completely eradicated, a remnant remains, only to resurface later.

We can resist the temptation to sin by turning to God for strength and choosing to obey his word. God tests people, but he does not tempt them by trying to seduce them into sin. God allows Satan to tempt people (see Job), however, in order to refine their faith and to help them grow in their dependence on Christ. The key is, a Christian accepts responsibility for his or her wrongs, confesses them, and asks God for forgiveness.

Don't let sin become deep rooted, turn to God when first tempted, so it can be easily weeded out before it takes complete control of your life.

Therefore, get rid of all moral filth and the evil that is so prevalent, and humbly accept the word planted in you, which can save you. James 1:21

Prayer

Father, who has taught us that we are all members of the same family, remove from among us all distrust and bitterness; and grant that we may live and work together in unity and love, through Jesus Christ.

Hymn

I want to serve the purpose of God
The Source, 256; *Songs of Fellowship,* 260

Dictators

Throughout history, there are numerous examples of dictators who have sought to control the world. All have failed in their quest, although at various times it has seemed as if they would succeed.

This century one particularly evil dictator was Hitler, whose hatred of Jews and other ethnic groups drove him to commit heinous crimes against humanity. Six million Jews were killed during the Second World War. Many were exterminated in concentration camps such as Auschwitz.

This is where people were turned into numbers and then ashes. The tragedy of the holocaust was caused by arrogance, not gas. It was caused by dogma. It was caused by ignorance. When people believe that they have absolute knowledge, this is how they behave. This is what men do when they do not humble themselves before God.

Science is a very human form of knowledge. We are always at the brink of the known, we always feel forward for what is hoped. Every judgement in science stands on the edge of error, and is personal. Science is a tribute to what we can know although all are fallible.

But science cannot give us absolute facts, it can only provide us with an insight into the wonders of God's creation. We cannot be the Creator. We have to cure ourselves of the yearning for unlimited knowledge and power. We have to close the distance between push-button order and the human act. We have to touch people.

When Simon saw that the Spirit was given at the laying on of the apostles' hands, he offered them money and said, 'Give me also this ability so that everyone on whom I lay my hands may receive the Holy Spirit.'

Peter answered: 'May your money perish with you, because you thought you could buy the gift of God with money! You have no part or share in this ministry, because your heart is not right before God. Repent of this wickedness and pray to the Lord. Perhaps he will forgive you for having such a thought in your heart. For I see that you are full of bitterness and captive to sin.' Acts 8:18-23

God placed us on the earth to exercise responsibility and not to seek power. We have a responsibility towards God, a responsibility to other humans and a responsibility towards his creation. Absolute knowledge is limited to God; in humans who believe they have it, it corrupts absolutely, leading to a world permeated by desolation and controlled by aspiring gods who place themselves above God Almighty.

History is littered with failed dictators who thought they had absolute knowledge and, therefore, absolute power and a divine right to intercede on behalf of the one and only true God. How wrong they were; how wrong future dictators will be. Trust only in God, the fount of all knowledge and power. Man is immortal but God continues for ever.

Prayer

Our Father, who art in heaven,
 hallowed be thy name;
 thy kingdom come;
 thy will be done;
 on earth as it is in heaven.
Give us this day our daily bread.
And forgive us our trespasses,
 as we forgive those who trespass against us.
And lead us not into temptation;
 but deliver us from evil.

Hymn

Make me a channel of your peace
The Source, 348; *Songs of Fellowship*, 381

Easter time

I have always enjoyed Easter. In general, it is the time of year when the weather begins to improve, the trees and flowers begin to bud, the daffodils are out, the days are getting longer and spring is on its way.

As a child, I enjoyed receiving Easter eggs, having time away from school, participating in 'bob-a-job week' and being given new clothes. In the north, it was traditional at Easter time to splash out on new clothes.

Like Christmas, it was also the time of year when families felt obliged to make an appearance at church, especially on Easter Sunday when it gave everyone the opportunity to make an impression in their new clothes. On Easter Monday, most families would go for a picnic and spend the afternoon rolling their hand-decorated hard-boiled eggs down the slopes of Rivington Pike or Parbold Hill, the local beauty spots.

Celebrating Easter would be quite meaningless if Jesus had died but had not risen from the dead. The whole point of Easter is to celebrate both the death of Christ and his resurrection. Over the years countless people have suggested that the events never took place and three main alternative versions of events which have generally emerged are:

The Jewish or Roman authorities took the body. However, if they had, they would have certainly produced it when friends of Jesus started to claim he was risen and alive.

Jesus' friends took the body. This would mean that they would have had to either overpower or bribe the soldiers; there is no evidence for this. Moreover, it is unlikely that the disciples would have later risked their lives proclaiming that Jesus was alive, if they knew all along that this was a lie.

God raised Jesus from the dead. Nothing else explains the many appearances of Jesus. For 40 days he appeared to his friends, usually in broad daylight and in a variety of places – in a room, on a road, by the sea.

Furthermore, nothing else explains the incredible change in the disciples. They had been scared by the death of Jesus. But now they became people full of joy and confidence. They went out into the market places fearlessly proclaiming that Jesus was risen from the dead and alive, the conqueror of death and sin. This is why the Christian faith spread so far and so fast and why millions of people from all backgrounds, countries and cultures worship Jesus as Lord to this day.

Prayer

Lord Jesus, help us to understand the sacrifice you made for us and to remember with joy that death was not the end and that you rose again on the third day; our Saviour and our Friend for ever.

Hymn

In the tomb so cold they laid him
The Source, 234; *Songs of Fellowship*, 245

Eighth commandment

The eighth commandment tells us that we should not steal. Yet in a test carried out by the *Reader's Digest* in which eighty wallets containing £30 were left around the country very few were handed in to the police with their contents intact.

The number of house burglaries continues to increase with nothing so distressing as someone having gone through your personal things, knowing something of your private life and having stolen objects that are precious to you.

Burglary, car theft and bank hold-ups are obvious examples of stealing. However, there are many other instances of theft that we tend to justify, and don't seem to put in the same category as the more obvious examples.

Tax evasion and claiming benefit payments when actually in work are two examples. We don't like to call this stealing, so we talk about borrowing, using shrewdness or playing the system. Society has this inconsistent view of stealing.

Just imagine what our world would be like if there were no stealing. Think how it would affect our relationships and our society if we could trust one another – no burglar alarms or complex security systems and everyone would be able to sleep at night, free from the fear of burglars.

Just think how society has had to change to accommodate the reality of stealing which goes on in our homes, shops, offices, schools, banks – even hospitals.

Greed is what makes us take what belongs to others. We imagine it will enable us to have a better quality of life. We have bought the lie that life is made up of what we own, wealth and possessions. We have a distorted sense of priorities.

Stealing also comes from a lack of responsibility, a refusal to see ourselves as part of a wider picture. We don't want to accept the level of personal accountability that we should. It is vital that we take a good look at ourselves to see where we are being dishonest; where we have taken from others in our family, in school or place of work. There may be many areas where we have to put things right, and we may stand out as different or odd, but changing society's views must start with us.

Help us all through today to obey our conscience and do what we know is right, so that we may do nothing for which we are sorry and ashamed at the end of the day.

Hymn

I was once in darkness, now my eyes can see
Songs of Fellowship, 263

Embarrassing moments

I was driving along the road the other day when I thought I recognised a friend walking on the footpath. As I slowed down and blew my horn, I suddenly realised that I didn't know them at all. You can imagine the embarrassment I felt – to get out of the situation I pretended to be lost and asked for directions to the hospital.

All of us will experience embarrassing moments at some point in our lives. For example I wonder how embarrassed you would feel in the following situations:

- Photos of you from four or five years ago being shown to relatives at a family party or everyone there being told how well you were doing at school.

- Being seen by your friends with a member of the opposite sex or being seen by your friends out shopping with your parents.

- Getting bottom marks in a test or getting top marks in a test.

- Making the alarm go off in a department store doorway or not having enough money to pay at the supermarket checkout.

The most embarrassing times are when you feel as if everyone knows that you alone have done something stupid! For example:

A person who had been asked to be a spokesman for the National Sleep Disorder Month overslept and missed a guest spot on the TV show *Wake up America*.

Police were called to a flat in Bournemouth after a passer-by heard screams of 'Help'. They found a 21-year-old in the shower, singing along to the Beatles' song of the same title at the top of her voice.

These are both situations where the embarrassment has been due to a simple mistake. But there is another kind of embarrassment you know you might feel when you have chosen to do or say something unusual you believe to be right and necessary.

People sometimes find it difficult to admit they are a Christian, or even show that they are interested in the Christian faith. They are afraid they will be teased or ridiculed and, as a result, embarrassed. Sometimes it's difficult to do what's right, especially if people react with mockery, false accusations and threats, belittling you in whichever way they can. It takes courage to stand up for what you believe in, but the temporary embarrassment will be a price worth paying for the Christian who is doing what is right.

Prayer   Lord, help us to proclaim our faith in you, and by acting out our faith bring those around us to also know you and your promised salvation for our lives.

Hymn   Stand up, stand up for Jesus
Songs of Fellowship, 513

Excess baggage

If you are like me, you enjoy going on holiday and visiting new places. However, there are two things that I dislike about going on holiday: packing and carrying the baggage.

If you have ever struggled through Reading station to catch the coach to Heathrow, you will realise how stressful this can be, especially when you are trying to balance five or six bags of luggage in each hand. There are always people who seem to get in the way, the doors are too small to go through, it's always raining, and the flight is usually delayed. Just at the wrong moment, that all-important strap holding a bag together breaks causing it to spill its contents as it crashes to the ground. To make matters worse you are advised at the flight check-in that you are carrying excess baggage and will either have to leave it behind or pay an additional charge.

Life is a little like this. Sometimes we carry excess baggage that causes us considerable stress and unhappiness. A common cause is not being able to meet the many and varied demands that are made on us. For example, as older pupils prepare for their exams they will have coped with a range of pressures: coursework deadlines, revision, homework, helping in the home, pressure from friends, acne, interviews, and so on.

For some people the stress caused by the excess baggage of worry leads them to give up or walk away from the problem – leaving behind their excess baggage. Recently a friend's son sought a solution by running away from home for a few days. He had been unable to cope with the excess baggage he was carrying. Only careful counselling on his return helped him to cope with the pressures he was under and place his concerns into perspective.

For some the solution is more radical. They turn to drink, drugs or crime; they become secretive and insular, ignore friends and family and shun any help offered. They enter a downward spiral of despair and depression seeing little of worth in their own lives.

There is a simple solution which is given us in the Bible. The book of Ecclesiastes advises people to work hard, and to enjoy the gifts of God as much and for as long as they can and offers hope in God that gives life its greater meaning. The author writes :

Everything that happens in this world happens at the time God chooses.
He sets the time for birth and the time for death,
the time for planting and the time for pulling up,
the time for killing and the time for healing,

the time for tearing down and the time for building.
He sets the time; for sorrow and the time for joy,
the time for mourning and the time for dancing,
the time for making love and the time for not making love,
the time for kissing and the time for not kissing.
He sets the time for finding and the time for losing,
the time for saving and the time for throwing away.
the time for tearing and the time for mending,
the time for silence and the time for talk.
He sets the time for love and the time for hate,
the time for war and the time for peace.

Ecclesiastes 3:1-18

God has set the right time for everything. He has given us a desire to know the future, but never gives us the capacity of fully understanding what he does. However, there is nothing better for men than to be happy and do good while they are still alive using the gifts that have been given them. All of us should eat and drink and enjoy what we have worked for. It is God's gift, let God take care of the excess baggage.

Whatever happens or can happen has already happened before. God makes the same thing happen again and again; there is nothing new in the world.

The message for us is that it is futile to become bogged down by excess baggage since no one will remember what has happened in the past, and no one in days to come will remember what happens between now and then. Although events may seem significant to us now, they are mere blips in a short and transient life.

Prayer

God grant us the serenity
  to accept the things we cannot change,
  the courage to change the things we can,
  and the wisdom to know the difference.
Reinbold Niebuhr (1892-1971)

Hymn

God is working his purpose out
The Source, 128; Songs of Fellowship, 135

Excuses

Do you ever find yourself giving excuses for not doing things you should have? I remember as a pupil I disliked the cross-country run on Friday afternoons after school. Each Friday I would try to come up with an excuse as to why I couldn't participate that particular week. It's funny how many times I had headaches, toothache, doctor's appointments, dental appointments, twisted ankles and upset stomachs on Friday, or how often bits of my sports equipment would mysteriously vanish on Friday morning and reappear by Monday morning.

Having taught for many years I've come across all sorts of excuses. These usually relate either to missing homework or absenteeism. For example on being asked why his homework had not been done, one boy said that the dog had eaten the pieces of paper it was written on. A likely tale, I thought – that was until the boy produced a plastic bag containing the chewed up remnants of his work which the dog had kindly spewed back up for him.

Or what about the pupil who told me that the cat had been sitting on the computer keyboard making the letter 'C' stick down, explaining their inability to finish the coursework on time.

Then you get the pupil who says they couldn't do the work. Why not? Because they couldn't understand it. Where is their attempt then? They haven't one. So how do they know they can't do the work?

How are we to know whether an excuse is genuine or not, particularly if we hear them all the time? Sooner or later, we have to take responsibility for who we are and what we do.

In deceiving ourselves and others, we are also attempting to deceive God. However, in light of God's all-knowing nature this is mere folly, for as Christ explained to his disciples:

There is nothing concealed that will not be disclosed, or hidden that will not be made known. What you have said in the dark will be heard in the daylight, and what you have whispered in the ear in the inner rooms will be proclaimed from the roofs. Luke 12:2-3

Are you one who tries in futility to hide your evil deeds from the One who knows the innermost workings of your heart?

Prayer

In all that we do, and all that we say, Father be with us as our guide and friend.

Hymn

I'm accepted
The Source, 217; Songs of Fellowship, 229

Expected or unexpected events

Talk

The start of a new year gives us the opportunity to take stock of our lives; to look back over the past twelve months, reflect on the opportunities and challenges that occurred and our response to them; and to look forward with anticipation to the next twelve months.

Some of the forthcoming events in our lives are already known. For example, sitting examinations, leaving school, starting university, celebrating birthdays, going on holiday, and so on. But there are some we don't know about. They might be happy or sad, wanted or unwanted, welcome or not so welcome events. For example, being expelled, getting into trouble with the law, the loss of a loved one, the birth of a baby, the marriage of a relative, redundancy, getting a job, being knocked over or coming into money;.

How we respond to the unpredictable happenings in our lives, particularly those that cause pain and stress, is influenced by what we believe. A fatalist assumes that whatever happens in life there is little they can do about it, and resign themselves to the inevitable. On the other hand, the optimist sees any event as an opportunity for growth and development, part of the life-long learning process.

Christians consider the major events in their lives – whether good or bad – to be part of God's plans for them. Although it is sometimes difficult for them to fully understand the significance of particular events, and the apparent inequity and injustice of the world, they are steadfast in their belief that God is always in control, there to guide and support them.

In Psalm 37 King David gave the following advice:

Do not fret because of evil men
or be envious of those that do wrong,
for like the grass they will soon wither
like green plants they will soon die away.

Trust in the Lord and do good;
dwell in the land and enjoy safe pasture.
Delight yourself in the Lord
and he will give you the desires of your heart . . .

. . . Be still before the Lord and wait patiently for him;
do not fret when men succeed in their ways,
when they carry out their wicked schemes . . .

. . . A little while, and the wicked will be no more;
though you look for them, they will not be found.
But the meek will inherit the land
and enjoy great peace.
Psalm 37:1-4, 10-11

To commit ourselves to the Lord means entrusting everything – our lives, families, jobs, possessions – to his control and guidance. Although we know what has happened in the past, the future is unknown to us. But there is certainty in knowing that the love and justice of God are always there to help us through both the expected and unexpected.

Prayer

Lord, help us not to miss any of today's opportunities, even when they are unexpected. Thank you for always being there to help us through both the good and bad times.

Hymn

I'm not alone for my Father is with me
Songs of Fellowship, 235

Facing the music

Talk

'Facing the music' is a term used when you have been caught doing something wrong and have to face the consequences of your actions.

Recently, there has been a court case where a famous author and politician was accused of perjury – a very serious offence which can result in a custodial sentence and heavy fine if found guilty.

It transpires that a few years ago a national paper accused the person of sleeping with a prostitute. The person successfully sued the paper for libel and he was awarded substantial damages. However, a few years later, leaked information suggested the person's personal diaries at the time had been altered to hide the fact that he had been with the prostitute. The replacement diary purported to show he was at a dinner on the date of the alleged offence, and therefore could not have been with the prostitute.

His personal secretary testified in the case and stated how she was instructed to obtain a new blank diary and to fill in false appointments to hide the person's indiscretions. In order to discredit the testimony of the secretary, the defence barrister played on the fact that during her time as secretary, she made false claims on her expenses.

The case illustrates how far we sometimes fall from applying God's precepts and standards to our lives. None of us can claim to be free from sin, and have, I am sure, during our lifetimes been economical with the truth. Perhaps, only through the grace of God, we have not ended up in court on serious charges. However, at some point in the future, we will, like the politician, be held responsible for our actions. And, although our sins may not appear as significant as other people's sins, they are nevertheless sins in the eyes of God.

The action also serves to show how our selfish actions can, and do, impinge on those around us. They too can become sucked in by behaviour that falls short of God's expectations. As Christians, we need to be very wary of this, and constantly on our guard. Unfortunately, Christians are sometimes perceived as easy prey, since they are known to be honest, true and open; they can be putty in the hands of a deceiver. The temptation of Christ by Satan shows us some of the arsenal available to catch the unwary Christian. The tactics of praise, power and flattery can be effective tools for catching Christians off their guard and leading them into temptation. C. S. Lewis further expands on this in his excellent publication *The Screwtape Letters*.

In it, Screwtape is an experienced devil. His nephew Wormwood is just at the start of his demonic career, and has been assigned to secure the damnation of a young man who has just become a Christian. Screwtape reassures his nephew that there is no need to worry, since many adults have, over the years, abandoned their Christian faith and joined them.

The point is, that lying and deceit can come back to haunt us like a ghost, our sinfulness impinges on the lives of others, and we are the target of attack by Satan, but in the end times we will be judged according to God's rules, and not by a human court.

As Matthew writes in his Gospel:

But I tell you that men will have to give account on the day of judgement for every careless word they have spoken. For by your words will you be acquitted, and by your words will you be condemned. Matthew 12:36

Prayer   Father, help us to be truthful to you and ourselves. So that on that day of judgement we will be able to hold our heads up high without having to 'face the music'.

Hymn   Give me life, Holy Spirit
Songs of Fellowship, 123

Fickle behaviour

Have you ever noticed how the presence of certain individuals can affect our behaviour? For example, when motorists are driving along the road and see a police car ahead, they automatically slow down, even though they were travelling within the speed limit prior to seeing the police car.

Pupils tend to change their behaviour when a teacher comes into view. They suddenly begin to tidy their appearance, stop running through the corridor, empty their mouths of chewing gum or pick up that piece of paper they have just thrown across the room.

It's as if people in authority, or perceived authority, are somehow able to influence our behaviour, even when they say nothing to us, or acknowledge our presence.

Does this mean that people adopt different behaviour characteristics according to the audience they have? Does it mean that people are not necessarily the person they appear to be, or do they put on different faces according to their perceptions of the importance of the people observing them?

How would we behave if there were a person of authority observing us all the time? Would we change our pattern of behaviour to match the expectations of the observer?

Christians strongly believe that we are always under the watchful eye of God who has high expectations of our behaviour, attitude towards others and general lifestyle. We believe that it is impossible to hide away from the watchful eye of God. Lifestyles should not be changed to accommodate the varying standards and demands of secular society, but must be a consistent application of God's principles outlined in the Bible. Christians must have commitment and discipline to serve, putting their faith into action, so that God, the authoritative observer, sees a consistency in our behaviour which matches his principles.

James, Jesus' brother, writes:

Do not merely listen to the word, and so deceive yourselves. Do what it says. Anyone who listens to the word but does not do what it says is like a man who looks at his face in a mirror and, after looking at himself, goes away and immediately forgets what he looks like. James 1:22-24.

Don't change your behaviour according to who you think is watching. Be consistent and true, since God is watching all the time.

Prayer

Thank you for providing us with the guidelines for right living, give us the courage to follow them consistently.

Hymn

O Jesus, I have promised
The Source, 391; *Songs of Fellowship*, 418

Firm roots

Jesus used many illustrations, or parables, when speaking to the crowds. A parable is a narrative of imagined events used to illustrate a moral or spiritual lesson. It helps us to understand spiritual truth by using everyday objects and relationships. Parables compel listeners to discover truth, while at the same time concealing the truth from those too lazy or too stubborn to see it. To those who are honestly searching, the truth becomes clear.

One of the famous parables is the Parable of the Sower. In this parable, Jesus talks about a farmer sowing seeds by scattering them over the ground. Some fall on the path where birds come along and eat them; some fall on rocky places where there is little soil, so when the plants grow they are easily withered by the scorching sun; others fall among weeds and thorns which grow and choke the plants; and the rest fall on good soil where they produce a good strong crop.

This is what the parable means: the seed landing on the path is like the word of God falling on the hearts of those that do not understand. The seed falling on the rocks is like the person who hears the word of God, receives it joyfully but forgets when trouble comes their way. The seed falling among the thorns is like the person who hears the word of God but eventually chooses to place their trust in wealth and materialism rather than in God. The seeds falling on the good soil are like those people who hear the word of God, understand it and act on it in their daily lives.

Experience tells us that what the roots of a plant are like, and what it feeds on, determines what sort of fruit grows. Where foundations are shaky, time and disaster will reveal it; where the simplest flaws are not spotted, dreadful disasters can follow – a basic defect in the fuel system of the *Challenger* spacecraft cost the lives of seven brave astronauts.

So it is with people. What we believe in our hearts will eventually determine how we live, how we behave and what we end up like. Everyone who hears the words of Jesus and puts them into practice is like the wise man that built his house on the rock and like the good soil that the seed fell on.

Prayer

Father God, help us to understand your words. Open our hearts to their meaning and give us the courage to put them into practice so that we have a solid foundation for right living.

Hymn

Bind us together
The Source, 51; *Songs of Fellowship*, 43

Food for life

We often take food for granted. When we go shopping, it is expected that we will find the shelves fully stocked and fresh fruit and vegetables in plentiful supply. The range of products is immense with a gamut of food from around the world.

It has not always been so. In my childhood, in the early fifties, the variety of food was very limited, especially fruits from abroad. Bananas, oranges, lemons and pineapples tended to be luxury items and the only apples available would be those grown in this country.

Pizzas, hamburgers, chicken nuggets and other fast foods we are familiar with today were unheard of. You were more likely to be familiar with dripping sandwiches, tripe and onions, or pig's trotters as part of the diet. The government were so concerned by this limited diet that they embarked on a programme of free school milk, daily doses of cod liver oil, malt extract and rose-hip syrup that was a rich source of vitamin C.

Different cultures and countries have different cuisines. The French are famous for escargot (snails) and frog's legs, the Germans for their sausage, the Norwegians for fish dishes, the Italians for pasta, the Indians for curries and the Americans for pecan pie. Similarly, different cultures eat certain foods at different times of the year, usually in connection with religious ceremonies or celebrations.

In this country, Easter is synonymous with hot-cross buns, Easter eggs and simnel cake. At the same time Jews eat special foods to celebrate the Jewish Passover. At this meal bitter herbs, unleavened bread, parsley and lamb are eaten to celebrate the liberation of the Jews from slavery in Egypt.

There are many references to food in the Bible. We are told in the New Testament about the miracle of changing water into wine and the feeding of the five thousand from five loaves and two fish. With his disciples Jesus uses bread and wine as symbols to represent the body and blood sacrificed on the cross. The breaking of bread and drinking of wine continues today as part of the Holy Communion services in all churches.

Jesus also talked about the 'bread of life'. By this he did not mean the food we need to keep physically well; he was speaking about himself, the One we will need to be spiritually well. Without food, our physical body deteriorates and dies, but without Christ our spiritual life is dead. However, Christ came that we might have life, and have it to the full.

As Jesus said:

I am the bread of life. Your forefathers ate the manna in the desert, yet they died. But here is the bread that comes down from heaven, which a man may eat and not die. I am the living bread that came down from heaven. If anyone eats of this bread, he will live for ever. This bread is my flesh, which I give for the life of the world. John 6:51

Prayer

God be in my head
   and in my understanding.
God be in my eyes
   and in my looking.
God be in my mouth
   and in my speaking.
God be in my heart
   and in my thinking.
God be at my end
   and at my departing.
Anonymous, Medieval

Hymn

Break thou the Bread of Life
Songs of Fellowship, 50

Forgiveness

There are times when forgiving someone for a particular wrong they have done to you is extremely hard. A few years ago a bomb detonated in Enniskillen, Northern Ireland, killed a young girl, Marie Wilson. She died in her father's arms. The next day a single word was telephoned, faxed and copied around the news agencies of the world. The single word became the headline of newspapers across the UK. The man was interviewed on television and later the Queen even referred to it in her Christmas broadcast of that year. The word was 'forgiveness'. Gordon Wilson said that he forgave those who had killed his child.

Forgiveness is an act, not a feeling. Though it may bring about feelings, forgiveness is an exercise of the will. When we forgive, we refuse to be further damaged by the wrong-doing of others.

A refusal to forgive is called resentment. And the victim of resentment is always the one who carries it. The people we refuse to forgive may neither know or care about our resentment.

To hang on to resentment is to harbour a grudge in the heart. By the minute and the hour, resentment steals the joy we could treasure now and remember for ever. We damage ourselves when we withhold forgiveness.

Such forgiveness is hard to grasp. We live in a world where we are used to earning things – money, position, and reputation, yet the words of Jesus could not be clearer: 'If you do not forgive those who hurt you, neither will your heavenly father forgive you.' At the heart of the Lord's Prayer is the plea, 'Forgive us our sins, for we also forgive everyone who sins against us.'

Sometimes it is hard to forgive because those who have wronged us show no regret; it seems at times that, given the chance, they would do it all again. In these circumstances it is important to understand what forgiveness is not. It is not saying to them, 'What you do doesn't matter.' When Gordon Wilson in Enniskillen said he forgave those who had killed his daughter, he was not releasing them from the fact that they will have to answer to God. He did not have the authority to do that.

In his letter to the Romans Paul makes this point very clear:

Do not repay anyone evil with evil. Be careful to do what is right in the eyes of everybody. If it is possible, as far as it depends on you, live at peace with everyone. Do not take revenge, my friends, but leave room for God's wrath, for it is written: 'It is mine to avenge; I will repay,' says the Lord. On the contrary, 'If your enemy is hungry, feed him; if he is thirsty, give him something to drink. In doing this, you will heap coals on his head.'

Do not be overcome by evil, but overcome evil with good. Romans 12:17-21

Prayer

Lord there will be times when we feel like extracting our revenge on those who have wronged us. Similarly, there will be times when we do wrong to others. We ask that you guide us to always do what is right and to give us the humility both to receive, and to give, forgiveness.

Hymn

Brother, let me be your servant
Songs of Fellowship, 54

Giving and love

Talk

February 14th is Valentines Day; a day when millions of people throughout the world give gifts of flowers, cards and chocolates to those they admire and love. I notice the Young Enterprise companies have been doing a roaring trade this week; especially with the sale of their roses.

The act of giving is a measure of the love we have for each other. This is not the type of love often portrayed in films and soap operas but the love that is underpinned by compassion, consideration and sympathetic sensitivity to the needs of others.

There is no end to the amount of love that we can give, or that can flow through us. Sometimes, however, we hold back from giving, from a sense of fear that we don't have enough to share. At other times we may feel that what we have to offer to others is not of much value or worth; so we curb our desire to be of service to others.

Instead of focusing on how little we have to give, we can decide to stop holding back, open up, and give freely from our hearts and out of love.

The following short extract taken from Corinthians describes the essential characteristics of true love:

Love is patient, love is kind. It does not envy, it does not boast, it is not proud. It is not rude, it is not self-seeking, it is not easily angered, it keeps no record of wrongs. Love does not delight in evil, but rejoices with the truth. It always protects, always trusts, always hopes, always perseveres. Love never fails. 1 Corinthians 13:4-8

Giving is about putting love into practice.

Prayer

Bless all families we pray, that parents and children may live together in love and understanding, and may in all things follow your holy words; through Jesus Christ our Lord.

Hymn

Love divine
The Source, 343; Songs of Fellowship, 377

God exists – but is not seen

When my oldest child was seven or eight months old, falling objects fascinated her. Unfortunately, her experimentation tended to take place in the early hours of the morning. Whereas I would be content to slumber on at this time of the morning, she was busy dropping rattles, cuddly toys, books, bottles and anything else that had been taken into her cot the evening before. I was comforted, however, by the thought that, to a certain extent (but not fully), she had inherited some of her father's scientific inquisitiveness – although wishing at the same time that it would manifest itself in daylight hours when I might be a little more appreciative of her efforts.

She was in good company, since 250 years earlier Sir Isaac Newton had pondered the reason as to why things fall and as a result had developed his gravitational theory. In this theory he describes how all objects attract each other with a force; when an object is dropped it is the gravitational attraction to the earth that makes it fall. Equally well, of course, it might be the earth is moving up to meet the object – but that is another story.

The interesting point of this is that although we cannot see the force between the object and the earth, we can see the effect of it on the object. Or to argue from the opposite point of view, since the object falls, there must be something moving it. This invisible force of gravity that creates very visible effects is responsible for many natural phenomena that we take for granted. For example, the daily tides, created by the gravitational pull of the moon on the earth, the orbits of the planets round the sun, and the parabolic path of a projectile fired at an angle above the earth's surface.

It is interesting to note how people accept the notion of an invisible force, acting through space, and producing tangible effects on the earth, whilst at the same time are unable to accept the existence of an invisible God.

Although we are constantly reminded of the creativity of God by the remarkable, and unfathomable universe in which we live, and the visibility of the wonders of nature, many are unwilling to recognise the omnipresence of God because he is not visible. Yet I would argue that he is made visible by the things that we can see. Just as we accept the invisible force of gravity by the effects we observe, because gravity is quantifiable and can be used to make predictions and to determine the trajectory of rockets, we are more willing to accept its existence.

But God is not predictable, and can never be, because this is a test of our faith in him. We have to make the unconditional decision that he does exist, even though he is hidden from our eyes.

For since the creation of the world God's invisible qualities – his eternal power and divine nature – have been clearly seen, being understood from what has been made, so that men are without excuse. Romans 1:19-21

Prayer

Almighty God, to you all hearts are open and all desires known. Purify our thoughts through your Holy Spirit, that we may love you with heart and mind, and praise you as we ought, through Jesus Christ our Lord.

Hymn

Immortal, invisible
The Source, 220; *Songs of Fellowship*, 234

Going convenience shopping

Over many years we have become accustomed to being able to shop when we want, at any time of day or night, any day of the week. Almost any commodity is available when we need it. Hence the phrase 'convenience shopping'; shopping which fits into our life-styles, meeting the demands of a consumer-driven society. One impact of this has been to encourage people to believe they have the right to services as and when they demand them, offering instant solutions for fast living.

This same attitude can sometimes spill over into our prayer life, where there is an impatience when prayers are seemingly not being answered, or where the purpose of prayer is directed to self-reward rather than towards what God wants. We arrive with a shopping basket of requests with the expectation that they will be fulfilled on demand. However, we need to step back and reflect on the motives of our prayer petitions and to consider whether it is reasonable to expect them to be answered in the way we desire.

This last point is an interesting one, since all prayers *are* answered, but not necessarily in the way we want, forgetting that God is the determinant in this matter. When we apparently do not receive the answer we want – for example, that new job – we assume that God has not answered our prayer, rather than perhaps appreciating that this is the answer intended by God.

We sometimes treat prayers like we treat convenience shopping – only using it when we have a particular need to be satisfied or met; for example, as we sit important exams, asking God for success, even though the rest of the time we ignore his presence since he apparently is an inconvenience in our lives when things are running smoothly and well.

In other words, there is a tendency to view prayer as a means of maintaining our lifestyles when we are being threatened by circumstances beyond our control. Just as the beauty of creation testifies to the power and love of God, as a loving Father he has a responsibility to guide and teach his children. If all our requests were fulfilled, no one was ever ill, disaster never struck, or there was no poverty in the world, our 'convenience God', would soon be forgotten and we would see no need to invite him into our lives. Yet history shows that 'Godless' societies lead to death and destruction.

When we petition God, it would be wiser to do so with humility, praise for his great works, seeking forgiveness for our sins, and asking him for direction in our lives so that we can live out his purposes for us. God is able to discern the motives of the heart and unlikely, as with convenience shopping, to respond to our every whim and fancy. There will be times when he needs to teach us, when he needs us to reaffirm our faith in him and to use us in ways we are unable to comprehend.

Be patient in prayer, they are always answered, but be prepared for *his* answers rather than those you desire.

Prayer

Father, we thank you for always being there to listen to our prayers and petitions. Teach us to have the patience to await your reply and the wisdom to understand your response.

Hymn

Have thine own way, Lord, have thine own way
Songs of Fellowship, 156

Good intentions

A few years after the Second World War the government decided to issue a quota of milk to all pupils each day to supplement their diet. The custom included giving one-third of a pint of milk every day to all pupils in schools. Not even exams could get in the way of this ritual. The Government, full of paternal concern, had decided that every young child ought to be provided for in this way. However, despite the good intentions, things did not always work out as planned. During morning break, milk monitors would walk up and down the aisles in the examination hall and pupils would take from the crate their bottle of milk with its straw sticking through the foil top.

You can imagine the scene: one hundred pupils in the hall all slurping their quota of milk from the bottle. In some instances, an unfortunate pupil knocked the bottle over, depositing its contents over the immaculately written page. Teachers gallantly tried to mop up the offending mess, leaving glorious streaks of blue-black ink across the page – ball-point pens were not in common use in those days. The distraught pupil added to the mess as tears rolled down their cheeks onto the page which now took on the appearance of over-cooked cabbage. What the markers thought of these scripts isn't known but I'm sure the scene was repeated throughout the country.

This nightmare scenario was often compounded by the fact that in May and June the weather gets hotter. The crates of milk would happily sit basking in the morning sunshine in the warmest corner of the playground, the temperature rising, before being delivered to the poor pupil for consumption. You can imagine the pungent smell emanating from the opened bottles. Even though you might have managed to avoid spilling the contents over your papers, you were almost keeled over by the acrid smell of rapidly souring milk – which you were required to drink. Occasionally a pupil would succumb to the combination of humidity in the exam hall and the stench of souring milk to brighten up their script by spewing forth their breakfast for all and sundry to see.

There are often events in one's life where good intentions have led to potential disasters and mess-ups. How many times have we come across the phrases 'I only meant to . . .', 'I didn't mean this to happen', and so on. But the fact that sometimes things don't work out quite as planned or imagined shouldn't prevent us from trying to do what is right.

Good intentions and consideration for others are the traits of those who follow the teachings of Christ. Sometimes these backfire on us as people reject our actions and motives, but this should not prevent us from carrying through those actions which we know are well intended and from the heart. We should take strength from the accounts of the apostles and early Christians who persevered despite considerable opposition to their teachings.

Although we might not be dishing out lukewarm milk to unwilling recipients we could find ourselves inviting unwilling recipients to drink from the fountain of life in Christ.

Prayer

Lord, help us to have honourable intentions and a faith that gives us the courage to persevere when things don't turn out quite as we wanted or intended.

Hymn

May we be a shining light to the nations
Songs of Fellowship, 389

Harvest time

The miraculous interaction between matter results in the production of food that sustains us. Without food, we could not survive.

We take for granted that when going along the shelves at our local supermarkets food will be available to buy – few of us make the connection between the seed that has been sown and the final product that we see on the supermarket shelf.

I remember, a good few years ago, asking one of my children where they thought bananas came from; the instant reply was, 'Tesco's'. There was no concept that they had to be grown on a plantation in a foreign country, harvested and then shipped to this country for distribution to the supermarket outlets.

The 'Big Bang' theory of the origin of the universe is well known – the theory suggests that the universe started out as a result of a massive explosion. It is difficult, almost impossible, for us to comprehend how out of the bubbling mass of matter, plant and animal life evolved. It poses the question of where the first seeds came from. How a seed can be produced without a plant to produce it and how a plant can grow without first starting out as a seed are unanswerable questions. It is indeed a miracle of creation and one which the hymn 'All good gifts around us' acknowledges as God's gift to us, something beyond our comprehension and understanding.

In his teachings, Jesus also made many references to farming and harvesting. He sometimes used these to illustrate the need for us to grow spiritually and in harmony with God's word. In talking to his disciples he talked of the harvest being plentiful but the workers few. By this he meant that there are millions of people in the world whose hearts have been prepared by God to hear the good news of the gospel, but that there are not many actually going out and preaching this good news to those people. The good news is, of course, that:

For God so loved the world that he gave his one and only Son, that whoever believes in him shall not perish but have eternal life. John 3:16

He talks about the good seed falling on the ground where some falls on good soil and flourishes and grows whilst others fall on poor soil and perish. Farmers will be familiar with the analogy in planting crops, but Jesus was saying that we should listen to the word of God for it is the good seed and from this we too can grow spiritually and in our faith and trust.

At the time of the harvest will you be ripe for picking or will you be rejected like the seed that has fallen on barren ground?

Prayer

Let your words be like ripe seeds in our heart.

Hymn

We plough the fields and scatter
Songs of Fellowship, 585

Having trust

The Greeks used to construct mathematical puzzles to help explain and explore the concepts of number and geometry. One of the most famous mathematicians was Zeno, who constructed three well-known paradoxes. A paradox is a statement that seems absurd or self-contradictory but may be true.

One of his paradoxes states the following: to go from any point A to another point B, you must first go half the distance from A to B, then half the remaining distance, then half the remaining and so on. Therefore you can never get from A to B however near A and B are. Therefore motion can never start.

There is a paradox here since we all have first-hand experience of setting out from one place and arriving at another. There must be some flaw in the argument which no doubt a mathematician could easily point out.

Zeno's paradox can also be used to illustrate why some people fail to achieve their potential. One common feature of pupils who fail to achieve their potential is the line of argument they give that says, 'I can never do that so I am not going to bother trying. I am not going to start because I can't get there.' There is an inconsistency in their argument, since unless they have tried something they will never know if they can get there or not.

The real problem is the fear of failure and damaged pride. No one enjoys failure although it is a necessary learning experience for all of us. Without failure we cannot grow intellectually, spiritually or morally. Those who place their faith in God know that human failure is part of his plan to strengthen our spiritual awareness and trust in him.

Jesus encouraged his people not to worry about the attitudes of others, or to be anxious or fear failure. He said that we should only fear God, not man; that God was more than capable of meeting our needs provided we placed our trust in him.

As Jesus tells us in the Bible:

I tell the truth, if you have faith as small as a mustard seed, you can say to this mountain, 'Move from here to there and it will move. Nothing will be impossible for you.' Matthew 17:20

Faith is being sure of what we hope for and certain of what we do not see. Hebrews 11:1

Ask and it will be given to you; seek and you will find; knock and the door will be opened to you. For everyone who asks receives; he who seeks finds; and to him who knocks, the door will be open. Matthew 7:7

Don't be like Zeno's paradox assuming you can't start because you can't get there. Place your trust in Jesus Christ who will show you the way.

Prayer

Thank you, Heavenly Father,
 for making us as we are;
 for hands to work and feet to walk and run;
 for eyes to see, and ears to hear;
 for minds to think, and for hearts to love;
 for all the people we know, and who know us,
 and for all those we shall meet as we go through life.

Hymn

Seek ye first the kingdom of God
The Source, 447; Songs of Fellowship, 493

Head in the sand

It is commonly reported that ostriches bury their head in the sand, hence the phrase 'bury your head in the sand' is used to describe the actions of someone hiding away from the realities of a situation. Everyone at some time finds difficulty in facing up to the big issues in their life and it is not uncommon for people to go into denial, pretending things haven't happened, by doing so hoping that problems will go away. It is rather like closing your eyes: since you can't see something it cannot exist.

Facing the realities of life can be stressful and painful especially when you are personally accountable for your actions. In schools, pupils often make up excuses or just deny all knowledge as they attempt to cover up for things that have gone wrong. As you get a little older and take on the responsibilities of a job and bringing up a family, it is not as easy to bury your head in the sand. With adulthood comes greater accountability and responsibility.

Do you feel fulfilled in your life, or do you feel empty and know that something is missing? Have you ever thought, or even hoped, that there is something after your time on earth? Or do you believe that death is the end of you? Perhaps you feel that there is something more, something better than what you have.

Most people would say they haven't the time to think about life. They are far too busy studying, working, making money or trying to enjoy themselves. Some people try to find fulfilment by burying themselves in their work or study; others want power and seek satisfaction in extending their influence; still others strive for riches, believing that money will provide them with everything they need to enjoy life. The truth is that these activities only succeed in covering their emptiness; by burying their heads in the sand they ignore the real issues of life.

One of the reasons for burying your head in the sand is the realisation that lives would have to change once you accept you are accountable to God and not material things. In reality, you should live the life he chooses rather than just doing as you please. Many people do not want to accept this, instead continuing to deny his existence. For them, it is not so much a case of 'I cannot believe', as 'I do not want to believe.'

Isn't it sensible to try to tackle the deep questions of life now, to face the big issues and stop pretending to be a human ostrich, burying your head in the sand? Shouldn't you find out if there is a God and if there is, shouldn't you find out if there is anything he wants you to do?

Prayer

Lord, help us to remember you are always with us, to ask for strength to do what is right and to turn to you for advice on our journey through life.

Hymn

It is good for me to draw near unto God
Songs of Fellowship, 253

Honesty

Talk

All of us at some point have lied. We may have had different reasons for lying; to keep ourselves out of trouble, to hide something which we know is wrong, to keep the peace, to prevent an argument, to start an argument, to get back at somebody, to help someone. A few years ago the phrase 'economical with the truth' entered the political arena to hide the reality that politicians lied. No one is free from the temptation to lie.

One of the reasons we struggle with integrity is because we look outside ourselves to explain faults in our character when the truth is we should be looking on the inside. Honesty is not determined by your circumstances any more than a mirror is responsible for your looks. What you see there reflects only what you already are and what you are is the result of the decisions you make every day.

Neither is integrity based on qualifications. Qualifications may get you a job, but only integrity will keep it. In ancient times, builders and artists used a personal symbol to mark the things they had created. This symbol was called their 'character' and the character of the person who made it always determined the value of any work.

Nor should integrity be confused with reputation. Reputation is what you're supposed to be; character is what you are. One is the mark of the moment, the other is the work of a lifetime.

Any time you compromise your integrity, you do yourself an incredible amount of damage, for integrity is your best friend. It'll never betray you or put you in a compromising position. It'll keep your priorities right and, when you're tempted to take short cuts, it'll help you to stay on the right road.

Integrity always puts character over personal gain, people over things, service over power, principles over convenience and the long-term view over the immediate. Every time you break a moral principle, it becomes harder, not easier, to act with integrity. Everything you've done in the past, including the things you've neglected to do, come to a head when you're under pressure.

As Solomon said,

Truthful lips endure for ever, but a lying tongue lasts only a moment.
Proverbs 12:19

Every day, you have a choice to make: either you bend your principles to conform to your actions or you bend your actions to conform to your principles.

Prayer

Give us your Holy Spirit so that we may know which way to choose, and which way to refuse; which choice to make, and which choice to reject; which course of action to take, and which course of action to avoid.

Hymn

Guide me, O thou great Jehovah
The Source 2, 708; *Songs of Fellowship*, 148

Hope in death

Talk

It is always extremely distressing and difficult to comprehend when a young person dies due to unforeseen circumstances or illness.

But even out of tragedy good can come. The untimely death has not been in vain and we should seek to take comfort from this:

- it has shown to us all that we must not take life for granted – we must take full advantage of each and every day that is given us;

- it has shown the importance of loving and caring for each other;

- it has drawn together families, friends, relatives and the community in a deeper understanding of the importance of relationships and the frailty of life;

- it has shown that we must take every opportunity to celebrate life and the achievements of others;

- it has given us a greater understanding of the plight of those across the world who are experiencing similar tragedies and sorrow and who are less fortunate than ourselves;

- it has brought us closer to an understanding of the meaning of life;

- it has humbled us and brought us closer to God.

Prayer

Father of all, we pray to you for those who have departed this life in faith and respect of you. Grant them your peace; let light perpetual shine upon them; and in your loving wisdom and almighty power work in them the good purpose of your perfect will; through Jesus Christ our Lord.

Hymn

Thine be the glory
The Source, 510; *Songs of Fellowship*, 551

Hypocrisy of the ad-man's lies

Talk

Society seems to judge a person's success in terms of their wealth, position and possessions. In fact, the media, television, radio, magazines and newspapers, extol the virtue of fat-cat salaries, luxurious lifestyles and outrageous living as they encourage their audiences, through not too subtle means, to aspire to these earthly idols.

In their wake an industry of greed, egotism and selfishness has been spawned; an industry that seeks to exploit the many at the expense of the few. An industry that encourages the 'I' culture, whilst marginalising the rest. A society that sits comfy with abject poverty and deprivation on the one hand and lives that are cluttered by non-essentials, clambering for an even greater share of the world's limited resources, on the other.

We justify our liposuction and cosmetic surgery on the backs of limbless landmine victims, we pout our obesity with indifference to malnutrition, we smoke our way to oblivion without a second glance at the children of TB, we smugly sip our refreshingly cool cokes in ignorance of cracked lips and parched throats that cry out for fresh clean water, we clothe our bodies with designer labels, drip wealth from our fashion accessories and hide behind democracy to justify the continuance of the lifestyle we relish. We have prostituted ourselves to the ad-man's lies, and shackled ourselves to consumerism and throwaway principles.

Are we not as guilty as the Israelites whom God punished for their ways? Have we forgotten the teachings of Christ?

Suppose a man comes into your meeting wearing a gold ring and fine clothes, and a poor man in shabby clothes also comes in. If you show special attention to the man wearing fine clothes and say, 'Here's a good seat for you,' but say to the poor man, 'You stand there' or 'Sit on the floor by my feet,' have you not discriminated among yourselves and become judges with evil thoughts? James 2:2-4

Christians have a commission from Christ to be witnesses in his name, to challenge inequity in the world and to live the truth rather than the hypocrisy of the ad-man's lies.

Prayer

Father, we thank you for sending Jesus to earth so that he could show us the way to you and eternal life. Let us not forget those less fortunate than ourselves and give us the courage to extend the hand of friendship as a testimony to your spirit within us.

Hymn   Who is he in yonder stall?
            Songs of Fellowship, 605

Inequalities

Talk

Many people enjoy reading the Sunday papers, spending most of the day browsing through the various sections.

It is interesting to note how the media often presents us with contrasting images of the world. Two recent ones spring to mind.

The first concerns wealth. In the colour supplement a woman is seen seated on what appears to be a chair constructed from bundles of money; she is obviously rich and successful. The caption reads, 'The lap of luxury – how much is enough to leave you sitting pretty.'

The accompanying article goes on to suggest that these days millionaires are ten-a-penny, but it takes more than £1 million to ensure happiness. The author writes, 'Money, money, money. Everyone wants it, wants more than everyone else, more than they have themselves. We all want it and we all want more.'

In the article a well-known restaurant critic worth about £70 million, is quoted as saying 'I cannot see the problem in having too much money, it can only bring joy.' The writer goes on to suggest that £5 million seems about the right amount of money we need in order to make us happy. In response, the restaurant critic says, 'Five million is a joke, I couldn't be happy with £5 million, I just wouldn't be able to maintain the lifestyle I am used to and desire.'

The second article offers a sharp contrast to the opulence suggested by the first. It is about war in Yugoslavia and carries the headline, 'Tragedy of refugees on escape route from death.' It contains harrowing scenes of a young Kosovar boy whose parents have been killed in the conflict by a low-level aircraft attack by the NATO forces on the makeshift convoy of refugees as they try to escape from the Serb forces. The bombing by the NATO forces was a tragic mistake but, as the caption poignantly says, NATO's apology will not bring the boy's parents back. A survivor of the tragedy states, 'I heard a very loud noise behind me and saw rubble fly everywhere. When I stopped and turned round I saw my wife, daughter and the neighbour lying dead, thrown on to the road.'

The articles raise some difficult questions. Why is it, if God is love, people suffer so much? Why doesn't he stop it all? This is an impossible question to answer. There is much in life that is a mystery and we have to accept we don't have the answers.

There is much about God that we cannot understand, simply because he is far greater in wisdom and power than we are. But as in other dark areas of life, the Bible sheds light. Without faith in God, the whole question of suffering and the inequitable lives that people have would become a meaningless tangle of knots.

First, suffering can come because of human sin. When God created us, he gave us the precious gift of free will. It is this which makes us human, enabling us to love and hate, help and hurt others. Without it we would be robots or machines incapable of love. But this great gift of free will has been used again and again for evil gains. What we do affects other people for good or bad.

Second, suffering can come because of human imperfection. No man or woman is perfect. Diseases and illnesses are all part of a sinful world and we are all subject to them.

Third, suffering can come because of human errors. For example, hundreds of children were born crippled because their mothers took thalidomide. God cannot be blamed for this tragedy or others that are the result of human carelessness or lack of knowledge.

Fourth, God sometimes allows suffering to test and strengthen our faith. The way we react in suffering will determine whether we are growing in faith or slipping back into doubts and resentment. We somehow have an in-built belief that God will always keep us from all accidents, illness, trials, temptation and sin.

It is not God but human weakness that has created a world of conflict, suffering and inequality.

Prayer

Father God, help us to be strong. Give us courage to face the future and to accomplish your plans for our lives. Let us see the pitfalls and dangers so that we can avoid them. Keep our minds and bodies free from sin and temptation.

Hymn

Now thank we all our God
Songs of Fellowship, 405

Is it all a lottery?

A survey carried out by *The Times* last year showed that for most teenagers one of their goals was to win the national lottery. Although the probability of throwing a six on a dice is 1 in 6, the chance of winning the national lottery is 14 million to 1.

It perhaps indicates the way in which money and the acquisition of material objects has become the main priority for many people. To a certain extent this may be understandable, since the media generally portrays success in terms of wealth and material possessions.

But if we are not careful, money may take control of our lives. It is not just the wealthy who can fall into this trap, everyone can be seduced into thinking that money and materialism are the panacea for all our troubles.

Unfortunately, or perhaps fortunately, when we die whatever wealth or possessions we have are left behind. Our lives on earth will not be judged in terms of the wealthiest people in the world, but in terms of how we used the money and possessions we had for the benefit of others. This will apply to everyone, irrespective of whether we had much or little.

Solomon had much to say on money and possessions. He writes:

Whoever loves money never has money enough;
whoever loves wealth is never satisfied with his income.
This too is meaningless.

As goods increase,
so do those who consume them.
And what benefit are they to the owner
except to feast his eyes on them?

The sleep of a labourer is sweet,
whether he eats little or much,
but the abundance of a rich man
permits him no sleep.

I have seen grievous evil under the sun:
wealth hoarded to the harm of its owner,
or wealth lost through some misfortune,
so that when he has a son
there is nothing left for him.
Naked a man comes from his mother's womb,
and as he comes, so he departs.
He takes nothing from his labour
that he can carry in his hand. Ecclesiastes 5:10-15

Now all has been heard;
here is the conclusion of the matter:
Fear God and keep his commandments,
for this is the whole duty of man.
For God will bring every deed into judgement,
including every hidden thing,
whether it is good or evil. Ecclesiastes 12:13-14

Solomon is telling us in this passage that those who love money seek it obsessively, never finding the happiness it promises. Wealth also attracts scroungers and thieves, causes sleeplessness and fear, and ultimately ends in loss because it must be left behind when we die.

Money in itself is not wrong, but loving money leads to all sorts of sin. Whatever financial situation you eventually find yourself in, don't depend on money to make you happy. Instead, use what you have for the Lord.

We should search for purpose and meaning in life, but these cannot be found in human endeavours and the accumulation of money and possessions.

Prayer

Father, we ask that you give us direction to know what the priority in our lives should be. Help us to fight against the false idea that somehow acquiring material goods and wealth will bring us greater happiness and closer to you. Teach us to understand your words and to fulfil your purposes for us.

Hymn

Fight the good fight
Songs of Fellowship, 107

It's good to talk

A few years ago one of BT's advertising slogans was 'It's good to talk'. The campaign was designed to encourage us to make greater use of our telephones to ring friends, relatives and family. In most homes, children don't need much encouragement since they already spend many hours on the phone. In fact, whenever the telephone rings in most homes, parents rarely bother to answer it since it is inevitably for one of the children.

It is one of life's mysteries how children are able to spend hours in animated conversation on a phone, yet respond with the monosyllabic grunts and stares of disbelief the moment parents wish to talk to them face to face.

Advances in telephone technology are only a small part of the communications revolution seen over the past twenty years. In the early days of telecommunication it was quite a status symbol being the owner of a telephone. Almost all people either made telephone calls from the bright red telephone boxes at the corner of the street or nipped round their friends to borrow the phone.

A few years ago, only a handful of people would have been mobile phone owners. Now they are almost as common as confetti. Although a mobile phone is useful, there are limitations. For example, the batteries fade when left on; it has to be within range; and, as with any phone, the person you are trying to call has to be in and has to want to talk to you. It is also costly to run.

However, you all have another mobile phone that's usable any time and at any range. It has free rental and there are no charges for calls. It's called 'prayer'. Christians think of prayer as being like two-way conversation, a bit like using a phone. We have to remember that this conversation with God needs to be two-way and we need also to listen to him, especially by reading his word, the Bible.

Conversation is part of a relationship, and prayer is part of our relationship with God. Like all relationships it needs working at. It's good to talk to God. This is what James has to say about the power of prayer as a means of communicating with God:

Is any of you in trouble? He should pray. Is anyone happy? Let him sing songs of praise. Is any one of you sick? He should call the elders of the church to pray over him and anoint him with oil in the name of the Lord. And the prayer offered in faith will make the sick person well; the Lord will raise him up. If he has sinned, he will be forgiven. Therefore confess your sins to each other and pray for each other so that you may be healed. The prayer of the righteous man is powerful and effective. James 5:13-16

Prayer

Jesus, give us the humility to acknowledge our strengths and weaknesses and to turn to you in prayer for our support and guidance, to give thanks and to offer our services to you.

Hymn

O God, our help in ages past
The Source 2, 905; *Songs of Fellowship*, 415

Journey of life

There is no doubting that God has a life-plan for each and every one of us; so much so, that he ensures we are provided with the necessary skills and attributes to fulfil this plan if we choose to do so. And this, I think, is a key issue.

Although God intended a particular direction for us, he is also a loving and caring Father who has given us the free will to make decisions on our own. If we had everything we desired or wanted, and no choices had to be made, we would soon forget the existence of God and why he created us.

How do we know when we are carrying out God's will? In some instances, we know, especially when it is a choice between right and wrong, since the Holy Spirit working through us, raises our consciousness to the difference between right and wrong. Almost all humans are born with an innate understanding of basic moral codes of practice.

However, in other situations we may experience uncertainty. For example, the choice of one's career. How do we know God's wishes? This is where our faith and trust in God is paramount. He calls us to respect and acknowledge him and consult him on all choices concerning our life. If we put to him, through prayer, the decisions we have to make, we must trust he will lead us in the direction that best lends itself to the fulfilment of his plans for us. This may, or may not be, the job we are seeking.

There may be different ways of knowing that God has answered our questions – just being in the right place at the right time, not luck, but intervention. Something out of the blue happening that confirms your choice, the intuitive feeling of having done the right thing and so on. On the other hand if we choose to go in a direction that we intuitively feel is not right, perhaps this should alert us to the fact that it is not what God wants.

There is, however, another option. God allows us to make incorrect choices in order to enable us to grow in our faith, knowing full well that the outcomes will not be those that we desire or want. God created man to serve and obey, but God is not completely autocratic and dictatorial, he allows for free will and choice because this can be used to test our faith and love for him.

As Christians become more pro-active in their faith, they experience greater self-fulfilment in their lives. Those that make decisions without reference to God often find their lives less fulfilling. God allows wrong decisions to be made in order that our spiritual maturity is assured in preparation for the challenges that God has lined up for us within his plan.

Some people never reach this stage, remaining obstinate and hard-hearted, failing to seek out God and, as a result, often experience unhappy and unfulfilled lives, cluttered with the material objects with which they try to camouflage the insecurity and lack of clear purpose for their journey through life that only God can provide when asked and listened to.

Prayer

Thank you, Heavenly Father, for all that makes life so interesting; for growing bigger and older and wiser, and for the new things which happen to us every day.

Hymn

Praise, my soul, the King of heaven
The Source, 433; *Songs of Fellowship*, 466

Keeping on target

If you want to be successful at doing something, it's important that you keep your eyes fixed on what you want to do and achieve.

It's important to keep your eyes on the road when you are riding a bike to avoid holes in the road or other road users. In a sprint race, the really good runners keep their eyes fixed on the finishing tape, and their heads never move until they have finished the race.

Similarly, it is important to keep your eyes fixed on where you want to go in life. It is easy, and often tempting, to waver from the route you need to take to achieve success. The road to success is never straightforward or easy, but unless you keep your targets and goals firmly in mind you are unlikely to reach the finishing line.

The Bible reminds Christians that to go in the right direction in life they need to keep their eyes fixed on Jesus. Paul wrote:

Let us fix our eyes on Jesus, the author and perfecter of our faith, who for the joy set before him endured the cross, scorning its shame, and sat down at the right hand of the throne of God. Consider him who endured such opposition from sinful men, so that you will not grow weary and lose heart.
Hebrews 12:2-3

The Christian life involves hard work. It requires you to give up whatever endangers your relationship with God, to run patiently, and to struggle against temptation with the help of the power of the Holy Spirit.

To live effectively you must keep your eyes on Jesus. You will stumble if you look away from him to stare at yourselves or at the circumstances surrounding you.

When you face hardship and discouragement, it is easy to lose sight of the final goal. But you are not alone; there is help. Many have already made it through life, enduring far more difficult circumstances than you have experienced. Suffering is the training ground for Christian maturity and growth. It develops your patience and makes your final victory sweet.

Prayer

Lord Jesus, forgive us when we let you down, and whenever we fail you, help us to try all the harder afterwards to live the kind of lives that you want us to live.

Hymn

Fight the good fight
Songs of Fellowship, 107

Leaving home

Talk

Every year, we see many thousands of students leaving home for the first time as they take up their places at university and college; and others who are embarking on their working career.

Moving away from home or starting work can be a distressing and lonely time – you are leaving behind the security and support of your family, meeting new people in strange surroundings – and the first few weeks can be lonesome as you manage on your own without friends and family to give support and security.

Each of you will at some point experience moments of insecurity and uncertainty especially when taking on new challenges. For example, starting a new school, a new job, or participating in your first trip abroad. Most of us take for granted the security of the environment in which we live, the predictability of our ordered lives. It is only at times when this harmony is disturbed by unforeseen events or changes to our regular routine that we become insecure and unsure.

But we should take encouragement from the fact that times of trial and separation from loved ones is a necessary preparation for the challenges of your life ahead. You can take comfort from the fact that by having a special relationship with God he will take care of you in all that you do and the circumstances that you find yourselves in.

As James writes in his Gospel:

Consider it pure joy, my brothers, whenever you face trials of many kinds, because you know that the testing of your faith develops perseverance. Perseverance must finish its work so that you may be mature and complete, not lacking anything. James 1:2-5

During those times of trial and separation place your trust in God and seek, through prayer, his guidance and support. He is always there whether you are at home or away.

Prayer

Father God, be our guide in all the things that we do. Let each new experience lead us closer to an understanding of your purposes for us.

Hymn

Like a river glorious is God's perfect peace
The Source, 866; Songs of Fellowship, 344

Life bearing fruit

To celebrate birthdays, wedding anniversaries, special occasions or as a thank you gift we often give bunches of flowers as a sign of our appreciation and love to the recipient. It is generally more common for women to receive gifts of flowers than men, who are, more often than not, the ones who give them.

Even though the flowers are fresh and colourful when they are given, their days are numbered. Within a short time, they begin to fade and wilt since they have been removed from their source of life, the rest of the plant. In a similar way, removing the branch from a tree causes the leaves to shrivel and the branch to die. It is no longer being provided with the nourishment from the tree it needs to sustain life; there are no longer any pathways to the minerals and water the branch needs to grow and flourish.

In John's Gospel we read:

I am the true vine, and my Father is the gardener. He cuts off every branch in me that bears no fruit, while every branch that does bear fruit he prunes so that it will be even more fruitful. . . . Remain in me, and I will remain in you. No branch can bear fruit by itself; it must remain on the vine. Neither can you bear fruit unless you remain in me. John 15:1-2, 4-5

In this passage, Jesus makes the analogy between the branches of the tree and the followers of Christ. He is saying that Christ is the source of spiritual nourishment for all his followers. Without his nourishment, like the severed branch, you will wither and die. The fruitful branches are the true believers who, by their living in union with Christ will produce much fruit.

Jesus knew that we were made for dependence on him, like the branch depends on the rest of the tree. He is our life-source, providing us with the spiritual nourishment we need. Although he is saying that we can do nothing without him, he is also saying that with him you can do everything he has appointed you for, including bearing much fruit.

Every gardener knows that periodically the branches of a tree have to be pruned. This allows them to become stronger and bear more fruit. Similarly in our life there are parts that need removing, a sort of spiritual pruning, thereby enabling us to grow stronger in our faith and trust of Christ and to produce a more plentiful harvest as witnesses to our faith in him.

Unlike the gifts of flowers, or the severed branches that soon wither and die, we need, through constant study of the word of God and prayer, to ensure that we remain firmly attached to Jesus, our only true source of spiritual nourishment and life.

Prayer

Father, through Jesus Christ, we seek replenishment of our spiritual nourishment so that we can remain faithful to you and fruitful witnesses to your name.

Hymn

Lord, you're faithful and just
Songs of Fellowship, 371

Listening and hearing

Over recent years we have heard a lot about genetically modified food and how it is possible to alter the gene structure. Genes not only occur in food but are carried by humans as well. The genes carry the physical characteristics through from one generation to the next. This explains why in some families the predominant eye colour is green and hair red, or why certain family members are short whilst others are tall.

There is much debate about whether genes are responsible for our personalities. If you are like my family, you might have heard comments such as, 'You're just like your grandma, she had a short temper too'; 'Your uncle never liked spending money either', and so on, the implication being that we have inherited personality traits from previous generations. In my own family, I am confident there is one particular gene that my children have inherited from their mother.

It is to do with listening and hearing. I have noticed that the children seem to have selective hearing, something in common with their mum. It seems that in certain situations they are unable to hear what is being said. For example, when I shout out that tea is ready all seem to hear and arrive at the table within seconds. But when I ask whose turn it is to wash up after tea, nobody seems to hear for I rarely receive a response.

Whilst sitting round the table I have tried different questions like 'Would anyone like to go to the cinema tomorrow?', or 'Does anybody need money?', these usually produce instant responses. It's as if certain combinations of frequencies and patterns of sound heard by the ears are incapable of translation into meaningful phrases. I don't think the condition is rare. I have heard reports from other parents who say they experience the same phenomenon with their own children, and husbands who say their wives appear deaf to certain questions. I am continuing research into this.

Sometimes all of us miss the message because we hear but don't listen. We all hear the word of God as written in the Bible, but how do we know we have listened to what is being said. The test is to examine the way in which we live and ask ourselves whether our lives are regulated by the word of God or controlled by human weaknesses. This is the hallmark of those who have listened and heard; it marks out the separation between self-centred living and life underpinned by God's word.

As Paul writes in his letter to the Romans:

Therefore, I urge you, brothers, in view of God's mercy, to offer your bodies as living sacrifices, holy and pleasing to God – this is your spiritual act of worship. Do not conform any longer to the pattern of the world, but be transformed by the renewing of the mind. Romans 12:1-2

Prayer

Caring Father God, we ask that you open our hearts and minds to your word and that we are able to show by our actions that our lives are a testimony of our faith and trust in you.

Hymn

O for a heart to praise my God
The Source 2, 904; *Songs of Fellowship*, 411

Love of money

Talk

The classified adverts and agony aunt columns make interesting reading in the weekend papers. The following extracts featured in one of the Saturday supplements recently:

- Alone again at 49: easy-going intellectual, romantic and loyal, medium build, 6', fair (yes, I have still got it all!) professional seeks companion to share the best things in life – intimacy, good food, wine, sun, travel. You? 40-55, race not an issue, sunny and good-looking, must genuinely enjoy the fulfilment of the quiet life as well as the fun times. Recent photograph appreciated.

- I'm an attractive brunette with a great sense of humour, 49, sensitive, caring, quick witted, practical and outgoing, 5'6", medium build. My interests include travel, cinema, theatre, entertaining and good food. I work in London centre and live in West London with my two children. Seeking a man who's attractive, solvent, sensitive, together with a sense of humour to match mine, up to 65. Photo appreciated.

- *Why does my cat eagerly wolf down my meaty morsels donated from my dinner plate, yet has to be in terminal stages of starvation before grudgingly nibbling at leading cat food brands?*

  The entire Darwinian point of cats is to make their owners' lives a misery – scratching the best armchair, moulting on duvet covers, refusing to be stroked by a loving child while rubbing against the legs of a confirmed cat-phobic, complicating holiday arrangements. I do not understand why anybody bothers with the wretched animals and would happily run them down were Mr Mills less squeamish. If you really want your animal to eat cat food, simply pile Whiskas onto your plate and tuck in; the perverse creature will demand to share it with you.

Although we might find these extracts amusing, there is something in them that illustrates to me the way in which, if we are not careful, our lives can be controlled by materialism.

In one we are shown how the cat hankers after something it does not have, but someone else has. In a similar way, many of us can fall into this trap, wanting what we cannot have or afford. Advertisements only succeed because they focus on man's greed and jealousy. They suggest that by not owning certain things we are somehow inferior, missing what is important in life. This has produced a society that is dominated by the acquisition of wealth and materialistic values.

The personal ads show that being successful in business or having wealth and the material trappings of life does not necessarily guarantee contentment or happiness. Each ad is really an acknowledgement that the person is unfulfilled in their life; they represent a cry for help, almost of despair. Outwardly, to their friends and relatives, the successful businessman or woman appear to have everything they could wish for. Money, fast cars, second homes, exotic holidays and good health but there is clearly something lacking in their lives which money cannot buy.

In the teachings of the Bible we are firmly warned against the two strands of greed and love of money. Neither will bring us happiness, but both can lead to corruption and ruin.

James, Jesus' brother, proclaimed the worthlessness of riches and material possessions. Today's money will be worthless when Christ returns. Although money by itself is not the problem, the love of money is. It causes some people to oppress others in order to gain more.

Now listen you rich people, weep and wail because of the misery that is coming upon you. Your wealth has rotted, and moths have eaten your clothes. Your gold and silver are corroded. Their corrosion will testify against you and eat your flesh like fire. You have hoarded wealth in the last days. Look! The wages you failed to pay the workmen who mowed your fields are crying out against you. The cries of the harvesters have reached the ears of the Lord Almighty. You have lived on earth in luxury and self-indulgence. You have fattened yourselves in the day of slaughter. You have condemned and murdered innocent men, who were not opposing you. John 5:1-6

This is a warning to all people who are tempted to adopt worldly standards rather than God's standards, as well as offering encouragement and hope to those oppressed by the rich.

Prayer

Dearest Lord, teach me to be generous;
   teach me to serve thee as thou deservest;
   to give and not to count the cost,
   to fight and not to heed the wounds,
   to toil and not to seek for rest,
   to labour and not to ask for any reward,
   save that of knowing that I do thy will.
St Ignatius Loyola (1491–1556)

Hymn

Thou, whose almighty word
Songs of Fellowship, 557

Master Builder

Talk

A few years ago I needed an extension built on to the back of my house in order to create a conservatory and a storage area for outdoor shoes and gardening implements. Since I was new to the area the only place to look for a suitable builder was in *Yellow Pages* and ring round for a few quotes

If you look in the 'Builders' section in *Yellow Pages*, you will notice that a number have a logo attached to their advert indicating that they are members of the Guild of Master Builders. This suggests that the builder is able to guarantee a professional job because he has satisfied the exacting criteria of belonging to the Guild of Master Builders. One would reasonably expect quality craftsmanship and construction of the highest standards.

When our extension was constructed, the master builder excavated a few tons of earth from the site and set about building firm foundations for the building because without them the extension would eventually crack and fail.

Through our lives, God calls on us to be builders of the church. By this, he doesn't mean physically building with bricks and mortar, but to spread his word and the word of the gospel to all who we meet. Through his teachings Jesus, the Master Builder, has given us a firm foundation on which we can build our faith and through which we can spread his word.

To illustrate this, Jesus taught about those who build houses on rock and sand, which is recorded in Matthew's Gospel and says:

Therefore, everyone who hears these words of mine and puts them into practice is like a wise man who built his house on the rock. The rain came down, the streams rose, and the winds blew and beat against the house; yet it did not fall, because it had its foundations on the rock.
Matthew 7:24-25

Is your life built on firm foundations or are you like the fool who has built his house on sand, which is easily washed away by the first trial that comes your way? Or are you following the example of Jesus, the Master Builder, in constructing firm foundations on which to build your life and spread his word to others?

Prayer

Loving Father, help us to seek the truth, the way and the light through you so that our foundations are secure enough to weather the storms and trials of life.

Hymh   Master, speak! Thy servant heareth
              Songs of Fellowship, 386

Mind your thoughts

The brain is a phenomenal organ of the body. It is capable of carrying out multiple computations far more advanced than the most advanced computer. Its filing system for recalling facts and figures is far superior to any of the mechanical or electronic systems we can develop. For humans, its degree of sophistication and development make it far superior to the brains of all the other members of the animal kingdom.

As people sleep, or just daydream, the brain is still active, producing thoughts that can sometimes be vivid and imaginative. All of us can recall with precise detail certain dreams that we have had. In fact, some people believe that the interpretation of dreams can reveal much about our psychological make up, whilst others claim that through their dreams, they are able to foretell future events or make predictions. Even when we are fully conscious or communicating with others our brains are busy analysing, interpreting, planning and making decisions; there is constant activity in the brain.

I wonder how you would feel if the thoughts you were having whilst talking to someone were flashed up on a screen for them to see. Would it condition the thoughts you were having, would it modify your thought processes? Just imagine the embarrassing situations it could lead to! For example, when you're telling someone how good he or she looks and your thoughts reveal that they look quite ridiculous in the clothes they are wearing. Or when you claim to believe an explanation being given, when in reality your thoughts reveal you think they are the biggest liars under the sun.

It is quite sobering to realise that although we can hide our thoughts from others, God knows what we're thinking. We should also understand that our thoughts determine our character since the thoughts that we hold in our mind help to form the aspects of our individual personality and make-up.

As Jesus taught:

But the things that come out of the mouth come from the heart . . . For out of the heart come evil thoughts, murder, adultery, sexual immorality, theft, false testimony, slander. Matthew 15:18-19

Although we can work hard to keep our outward appearance attractive, what is in our hearts is even more important and matters much to God. We should be constantly asking ourselves whether our thoughts are pure and wholesome, driven by a desire to please God and a true reflection of who we really are and want to be.

Prayer

Lord, let the words from our mouths, and the thoughts in our hearts, be pleasing to you now and always.

Hymn

Be thou my vision
The Source, 50; *Songs of Fellowship*, 42

Money and competing priorities

Talk

Some of you may have seen the headline in the papers a while ago about a famous singer having spent £40 million in 20 months. Included in his spending spree were:

£293,000 on flowers
£4 million on jewellery
£2 million on cars
£121,000 spent on celebrating his fiftieth birthday

and many other luxury items that suit a person who has fallen in love with himself and his money and appears out of touch with the real world.

On Friday, there was an incident after school, which was also linked to money and people's attitudes towards it. Five boys, on the way home from school, came across a moneybag that had been dropped on the forecourt of a petrol station. On looking inside the bag, they discovered to their amazement over £3,000 in cash.

It is a testimony to their honesty and integrity that they returned to school and handed the money in. Its owner was later tracked down and found to be a local businessman who, after filling up with petrol earlier in the day, had accidentally dropped the money-bag on the forecourt. The five boys received £20 between them as a reward. The school is immensely proud of them; many others would have been tempted to keep the money.

It is reassuring to know that unlike the self-centred singer or the mean businessman the boys can hold their heads high in full knowledge that what they did was right in the eyes of God and although their reward may not be all that tangible in this world it will be in the next.

I suspect that the singer's and businessman's true God is money but, as we are warned in Matthew's Gospel, we need to be wary of the dangers of this since money and possessions can have a habit of controlling our lives. As Jesus said:

Do not store up for yourselves treasures on earth, where moth and rust destroy, and where thieves break in and steal. But store up for yourselves treasures in heaven, where moth and rust do not destroy, and where thieves do not break in and steal. For where your treasure is, there your heart will also be. Matthew 6:19-21

Have you got your heart in the right place?

Prayer

Lord, help us today not to let anyone or anything stop us from being what we ought to be and doing what we ought to do.

Hymn

Father, you are my portion
The Source, 104; *Songs of Fellowship*, 103

Never trust the packaging

One of the new food products to come onto the market in recent years is an orange drink produced by manufacturers of washing powder. In the last year its sales have increased by 5224 per cent to £160 million.

The packaging and adverts suggest that the orange drink is a healthy fresh fruit drink. In fact, it is full of thickeners, colours and flavourings to make it look like a fruit juice, when in fact it's a very sugary drink with less nutritional value than well-known fizzy drinks.

Meaningless words are often stuck on products to persuade us to buy them. The packaging often hides the inferior quality of the product contained within it.

The same is often true with people. People are seldom as they first appear. Your first impressions are always limited and possibly wrong. Packaging can be very deceptive. Cereal boxes can make drab cereal look the most exciting food on earth. It doesn't follow that a well-dressed person is a better person than someone who cannot afford to dress as expensively.

Today's society seems more concerned with the packaging and image than the product itself. Images on television convey the message that a successful person, and by implication a better person, is the one who displays the outward signs of that success; whether it's by the clothes they wear, the food they eat, the cars they drive or the books they read.

A study of the words and actions of Jesus in the Bible shows us that he always considered the inner being more important than the external packaging, he sought what was beneath the outer veneer; searching out what was good or what needed changing. James gives the following advice to Christians:

My brothers, as believers in our glorious Lord Jesus Christ, don't show favouritism. Suppose a man comes into your meeting wearing a gold ring and fine clothes, and a poor man in shabby clothes also comes in. If you show special attention to the man wearing fine clothes and say, 'Here's a good seat for you', but you say to the poor man, 'You stand there' or 'Sit on the floor by my feet', have you not discriminated among yourselves and become judges with evil thoughts? James 2:1-4

Never include or eliminate people from your life based on their appearance.

Prayer   Father, we ask you for the maturity not to judge others by their outward appearance, but to focus on their hearts and minds. In our dealings with others help us to bring them to know you as an intimate friend and guide.

Hymn   Give thanks
The Source, 118; *Songs of Fellowship*, 124

On the road to life

One piece of software available these days is a programme able to calculate the possible routes between any two places in the UK. For example, if I want to travel from here to Brighton, all I have to do is type in my start and end points for the journey and the computer does the rest.

In calculating the route there are a number of options available. For example, the types of roads I want to use, e.g. A roads, B roads or motorways. It asks if I want to stop to visit various places of interest, and what I want the average speed of the journey to be. Having provided the information the software works out the various possibilities and prints out directions about the route. It only does this provided I am clear about where I want to go and where I am coming from.

I have used the software on a number of occasions and for the most part it has been successful in navigating me from one place to another. On other occasions, it has been less successful because it has been unable to anticipate the hold-ups due to accidents or detours due to roads being closed. Although these have caused inconvenient delays on the journey, I have always managed to arrive safely.

Our journey through life is a little like going from one place to another, the ups and downs sometimes causing us to stop to reflect about where we are going and how we are getting there. The journey is often bumpy, presenting us with challenges, hurdles and detours; for example, the birth of your first child, the loss of a loved one, securing your first job, being made redundant, getting married, being divorced, passing examinations, failing an interview and so on.

These life challenges can often raise concerns in our minds about the purpose and meaning of life, testing our faith in, and understanding of, God. On this matter Jesus said to his disciples:

Therefore I tell you, do not worry about your life, what you will eat; or about your body, what you will wear. Life is more than food, and the body more than clothes. Matthew 6:25

Who of you by worrying can add a single hour to his life? Since you cannot do this very little thing, why do you worry about the rest? Luke 12:26

Jesus challenges us to think beyond earthbound goals and to use what we have been given for God's kingdom. Faith, service and obedience are the way to become rich towards God.

Jesus commands us not to worry. Only faith in God can free us from anxiety in our earthbound lifelong journey to salvation.

Prayer

Lord, grant us sufficient strength, faith and protection to guide and support us through all of life's dangers and temptations. Keep us on the narrow road to eternity.

Hymn

I am a wounded soldier
Songs of Fellowship, 198

Our source of strength

Diamond is the hardest natural substance known to man. Its remarkable strength comes from the way in which the carbon atoms in it bond, in a three-dimensional array, with other carbon atoms. Graphite, on the other hand, is a relatively soft material, even though it, like diamond, consists of carbon atoms. The difference in their properties lies in the fact the carbon atoms within graphite only form bonds with other carbon atoms that are in the same plane, whereas those in diamond are bonded within a three-dimensional structure. So, although diamond and graphite are composed from the same basic element, carbon, they have remarkably different physical characteristics. The one substance is characterised by three dimensions and the other by two dimensions.

Forging strong three-dimensional links is a characteristic of Christians. They endeavour to forge a bond between themselves, the Holy Spirit, God and Christ. This is not a one-dimensional relationship, but one that is multi-dimensional. Through it, Christians find an inner strength that is not easily broken or shattered.

In a largely secular society relationships that exist are often confined to earthly dimensions, lacking a spiritual dimension, which, in addition to giving added strength, affords a three-dimensional perspective of life. In placing their trust in others, or through material objects, many people fail to discover the inner strength that the spiritual dimension can bring to their lives. As a result they often crumble and fall apart under excess pressure and stress brought on by the many demands of the modern world. Friends and relatives often let them down when they need them most, businesses fail, marriages falter, illness saps their inner strength and the props of alcohol, drugs and other outlets are often used to try and compensate for and repair the inherent weaknesses of the bonds between themselves and others.

In placing their trust and faith in Christ, God and the Holy Spirit, Christians are able to draw on unlimited support and encouragement. It is not unusual to observe how those at one with Christ have an inner calm and peace, often at odds with those around them. Whilst Christians and non-Christians are essentially composed of the same elements and atoms, the major difference in their lives is the way in which Christians have developed between themselves and God the strongest bonds known to man; by expressing their faith in Christ and asking for their weaknesses to be forgiven, the ties they make cannot be broken by any human means.

It is this inner strength that over the centuries has given many martyrs to the Christian faith the will to continue and complete their work for God. Let Christ enter your life; allow him to bring to it a three-dimensional perspective thereby ensuring everlasting bonds of infinite strength and sustainability that will carry you through life to eternity.

Even the strongest people get tired at times, but God's power and strength never diminishes. He is never too tired or too busy to help and listen. His strength is our source of strength.

When you feel all of life crushing you and cannot go another step, remember that you can call upon God to renew your strength.

Hoping in the Lord is expecting that his promise of strength will help us to rise above life's distractions and difficulties. It also means trusting in God. Trusting helps us to be prepared when he speaks to us. Then we will be patient when he asks us to wait and expect him to fulfil the promises found in his word.

Prayer

O God, our Father, thank you for the world in which we live.
Thank you
    for all the beautiful things in it;
    for all the interesting things in it;
    for all the useful things in it.

Thank you for the life which you have given us.
Thank you for
    our bodies to act;
    our minds to think;
    our memories to remember;
    our hearts to love.

Thank you for giving us
    so many things to enjoy;
    so many things to learn;
    so many things to do;
    so many people to love.

Help us never to do anything which would make the world uglier or people sadder.

Help us always to add something to the world's beauty and to the world's joy: through Jesus Christ our Lord.

Hymn

Fight the good fight
Songs of Fellowship, 107

Out of place

Talk

I wonder if any of you have ever found yourselves the odd one out. How does it feel? Do you feel embarrassed, intimidated, insecure, worried, threatened, isolated . . .

There are many situations where this can occur in our daily lives. For example you might be:

- the new person in the class

- tall, thin, fat, spotty

- the one who holds different opinions from the rest

- the only one who has done their homework

- the only one who has not done their homework

- the only one without a boy- or girlfriend

- old, blind, crippled, deaf or disabled

I am sure that all of you can think of someone who stands apart from the rest – for any number of reasons.

Try and imagine being them – what is it like to be in someone else's skin. To think like they do, to feel like they do. Of course we can only imagine it.

There is a lot of misunderstanding in the world, a lot of hurt, a lot of fighting, because we only look at things from our own point of view. We don't take time to consider what the other person is thinking or feeling. The world can be a selfish place – only thinking of ourselves. The apostle Paul in his letter to the Galatians highlights the need to be good to all and avoid selfishness.

Do not be deceived: God cannot be mocked. A man reaps what he sows. The one who sows to please his sinful nature, from that nature will reap destruction; the one who sows to please the Spirit, from the Spirit will reap eternal life. Let us not become weary in doing good, for at the proper time we will reap a harvest if we do not give up. Therefore, as we have opportunity, let us do good to all people, especially to those who belong to the family of believers. Galatians 6:7-10

Prayer

Lord, help us to appreciate the skills and talents of all those we meet in our daily lives.

Hymn

The church's one foundation
The Source, 477; Songs of Fellowship, 526

Painting by numbers

When I was much younger, I used to enjoy those painting by numbers kits. I suppose it allowed me to pretend that I was a great artist.

Usually I would begin the painting by filling in all the spaces with the intense colours – the reds, the yellows and the blues. At this stage, the painting would look rather ordinary and two-dimensional. Eventually I would be left with just one colour to add – black, some would argue the most boring colour.

But the moment it was applied the effect it produced was remarkable. Suddenly the painting would spring to life and snap into three dimensions. Instead of being uninteresting, the whole picture became rich and dynamic, with depth, subtlety and drama.

Life is a little like this. It's the darkness, the shadows, the difficult things that can give shape, form, and ultimately colour to the canvas of our lives.

If there are no shadows, no black patches, no grey areas, then our view of life tends to be bland, uninteresting, superficial, with little depth to it. We become preoccupied with the trivia. But sometimes, we experience the periods of pain, depression, uncertainty, adversity, sorrow, anguish, illness, the loss of loved ones. Without them our life would be the poorer; their presence brings out the colours in life; they can, and often do, bring out the best in us. They help focus our minds on the important issues, putting things into perspective. They help us to raise those important questions which most of the time we ignore or refuse to acknowledge.

All too often we clutter up our lives with unimportant issues, wasting our time in the process. Having a fatal illness forces us to think about what is important in life. Pain and illness in our life tends to help us grow spiritually. We are told in the Bible that God will prune us in order to make us bear more fruit. The process of pruning is likely to be painful.

So if at the moment you are going through difficulty, pain, loss, loneliness, depression or sadness, pause to think that what currently you find to be a stumbling block may later become a stepping stone, or even a cornerstone for your future Christian life.

God knows all about it, and in it he has plans for you, which are for the very best – and they are good.

The following is taken from James' Gospel. James was the brother of Jesus and a Jew. His Gospel was written around AD 45. During Christ's lifetime James was a non-believer.

Consider it pure joy, my brothers, whenever you face trials of many kinds, because you know that the testing of your faith develops perseverance. Perseverance must finish its work so that you may be mature and complete, not lacking anything. James 1:2-4

Prayer

May the presence of God in our lives lighten our darkness, guiding us during those times of trial and in so doing enable our faith and understanding to grow.

Hymn

Like a river glorious is God's perfect peace
The Source 2, 866; *Songs of Fellowship*, 344

Personal manager

A good few years ago there used to be an advert for one of the High Street banks which showed a young couple at home discussing their finances. At some stage in their discussions, one of them opened a door to a cupboard in the room and out stepped the bank manager to give them advice. The inference was that with this particular bank help was always available, it would be like having your very own bank manager in your home all the time. This was a ludicrous suggestion, unless of course you happened to belong to a family where one of the adults was indeed a bank manager.

There are many situations in our everyday lives where we need to seek help, reassurance, guidance and support. As young adults you can turn to parents, older brothers or sisters, other adults, friends or relatives for their support and assistance, and in school, teachers are available to help and guide pupils through periods of uncertainty or insecurity.

There will be times, however, where you may not feel comfortable talking to anybody else about your concerns and inner thoughts. For example, when you might be confused about the meaning of life, what your purpose here on earth is; when you are feeling rejected or have low self-esteem; when things are happening to you that are not right; when you harbour innermost secrets.

Imagine what it would be like if at these times you could open a door in your room to consult with your very own manager – a bit like the bank manager mentioned earlier. This manager would be responsible for advising on all aspects of your life. They would be there at the good times, to help with your celebrations, and at the low points to encourage and guide you. They would be able to answer questions about any aspect of your life.

Most people would find this an invaluable service, something which they wouldn't want to discard once they had used it.

The interesting thing is that many millions of people throughout the world have this manager available already but very few use it effectively to answer life's questions or allow it to manage the way in which they conduct their lives. Often referred to as the Book of Life, the Bible contains all the answers that we need to know. It can be a source of comfort, a source of inspiration, it can challenge our lifestyles and offer solutions to our problems. But unlike the bank manager in the cupboard it is most effective as a manager when it is used every day, not just pulled out at the difficult times.

A daily reading from the Bible can be instructional and inspirational, it can set the tone for the day and help you prepare in a quiet way for the trials that may come your way. The reason it can do this is because the Bible is the word of God which is the truth, the way and the life. The following reading from the Bible written by Paul talks of the importance of the scriptures for our daily life. It is taken from 2 Timothy which was the last letter written by Paul before being executed by the Romans for his faith.

But mark this: There will be terrible times in the last days. People will be lovers of themselves, lovers of money, boastful, proud, abusive, disobedient to their parents, ungrateful, unholy, without love, unforgiving, slanderous, without self-control, brutal, not lovers of the good, treacherous, rash, conceited, lovers of pleasure rather than lovers of God – having a form of godliness but denying its power. Have nothing to do with them. . . . All Scripture is God-breathed and is useful for teaching, rebuking, correcting and training in righteousness, so that the man of God may be thoroughly equipped for every good work. 2 Timothy 3:1-5, 16-17

Prayer

Almighty God, give us wisdom to perceive you, intellect to understand you, diligence to seek you, patience to wait for you, vision to behold you, a heart to meditate upon you, and life to proclaim you.

Hymn

Lord, have mercy on us, come and heal our land
The Source, 328; Songs of Fellowship, 354

Passing the buck

Over recent years, there has been an increasing shift towards the 'no blame culture'. By this I mean that as a society we have become increasingly adept at blaming others for our mistakes, our behaviour and our failures. Reading court transcripts reveals lawyers increasingly using 'no blame' arguments to defend the illegal, and often horrendous, actions of others.

For example, physically attacking a defenceless old-age pensioner is justified in terms of the disadvantaged childhood the defendant experienced. A murder is justified because the defendant experienced no love in the foster home they were brought up in. The stealing of other people's property is justified because the defendant was emotionally scarred, having been brought up in extreme poverty. Increasingly, people are justifying their actions because of some trauma in their past. For example, they may have been bullied, physically or mentally abused, experienced a deprived childhood, extreme poverty, or any other psychological or sociological occurrence in the past.

Undoubtedly, many people do experience traumatic events in their lives that leave them with deep psychological scars which require careful counselling to heal. However, they cannot be used to justify wrongful acts now. There is a tendency for people to hide behind the 'no blame culture' in order to avoid taking responsibility for their actions, and it has spawned a whole industry of quacks, and charlatans more keen on making huge profits than on seeking justice and accountability.

The teachings in the Bible are quite clear on this issue. We each have been given the free will to act as we wish, but at the same time, we will each be judged according to our actions by God. Although, whilst on earth, we may be able to escape punishment by the clever manipulation of the system, in God's eyes we will be guilty if we have broken his laws and commands.

There is an opportunity, through Jesus Christ, to repent our sins and seek forgiveness. Jesus died on the cross so that we might do this and be saved. However, those who do not turn in faith to Christ will, on the final judgement day, be condemned when God will judge them. He will hold each of us accountable for our actions and there will be no opportunity for mitigating circumstances that try to shift the blame to others.

Are you ready to stand by your actions; have you the courage to accept responsibility for the times when you have done wrong, have you placed Christ at the centre of your life?

Jesus teaches about prejudice in the following passage from Luke's Gospel:

Do not judge, and you will not be judged. Do not condemn, and you will not be condemned. Forgive, and you will be forgiven. Give, and it will be given to you. Luke 6:37-38

No good tree bears bad fruit, nor does a bad tree bear good fruit. Each tree is recognised by its own fruit. People do not pick figs from thorn-bushes, or grapes from briers. The good man brings good things out of the good stored up in his heart, and the evil man brings evil things out of the evil stored up in his heart. For out of the overflow of his heart his mouth speaks. Luke 6:43-45

Prayer

Thank you, Lord, for bringing us safely to the start of this day. Help us to accept the individuality of our friends, family and acquaintances; keep our hearts and minds open so that we are not prejudiced in our dealings with them. Through Jesus Christ our Saviour.

Hymn

Make me a channel of your peace
The Source, 348; *Songs of Fellowship*, 381

Protection

The British have a tendency to go mad when the sun comes out. Like lemmings they rush to the seaside or get the barbecue out hoping to capture the rays as a further deposit to their annual summer tan.

However, the sun's rays are capable of harming us. For example, infrared can give third-degree burns giving the appearance of a freshly boiled lobster, whilst ultra-violet can cause skin cancer. Staring directly at the sun can cause permanent damage to the retina and lead to blindness. It seems rather strange that the sun, so essential to life, can also destroy us.

Sensibly, when we are out in the sun we take precautions to protect our bodies from the harmful rays. Sun cream is used to block out the ultra-violet, light reflective clothing to protect us from the infrared rays and Polaroid glasses to reduce the intensity of light entering our eyes.

However, the sun is not the only potentially dangerous source we come across. Every day the body fends off bacteria, germs, dust, dirt, acid, etc., the systems it has in place are able to protect us from unwanted and harmful substances. For example, the liver is used to filter out unwanted toxins and chemicals from the blood and our eyelashes stop foreign matter from entering our eyes.

But as with all defences they can be easily destroyed or rendered ineffective by the habits we acquire – for example smoking, taking drugs or drinking to excess. These can be harmful to our bodies and are capable of destroying the very organs designed to filter out, and protect us from, unwanted and harmful substances.

Whilst our bodily organs can protect us physically, how can we protect ourselves from the experiences of life that lead to spiritual decay, that result in a blurring of the edges between right from wrong? Whilst bodily organs function to protect the physical well-being, they are not designed to protect us from spiritual decay.

The answer is not to be found in terms of prescribing any specific medication or protective clothing but in terms of our relationship with God. We often depend on our own skills and abilities when life seems easy, but we turn to God when we feel unable to help ourselves. Depending on God is a realisation of our need for spiritual protection and of our own powerlessness. Paul gives the following advice:

Finally, be strong in the Lord and in his mighty power. Put on the full armour of God. In addition to this, take up the shield of faith, with which you can extinguish all flaming arrows of the evil one. Take the helmet of

salvation and the sword of the Spirit, which is the word of God.
Ephesians 6:10-17

Prayer

Father God, we ask that you help our faith in you to grow. Protect us from those experiences that lead to a spiritual wilderness so that, in time, we might also enjoy everlasting life with you.

Hymn

Soldiers of Christ, arise, and put your armour on
Songs of Fellowship, 506

Purpose, power and peace

Talk

Over the years, there have been many examples of famous personalities remaining deeply unhappy and confused despite all the trappings that go with wealth and stardom. It is as if something is missing in their lives. Occasionally their despair and unhappiness drives them to seek solace in alcoholism and drugs and in a few extreme cases to commit suicide. Despite this, many people throughout the world continue to hanker for fame, power and fortune.

A thousand years ago, it is recorded in the Bible that God offered to grant the king of Israel anything he wanted. Now you might imagine, given this opportunity, there would be the temptation to seek fame, fortune and power. But in this case King Solomon sought only wisdom. The wisdom to know the difference between right and wrong and the wisdom to lead the people of Israel in the ways of the Lord. You may recall that Solomon is famous for writing some of the 3000 proverbs and sayings that are still in use today.

Solomon didn't place his trust in material possessions, in wealth, fame or fortune. Instead, realising that these were only temporary things, he placed his trust in God to direct and lead him and, in return, asked for wisdom to understand God's word and put it into practice.

This didn't mean that Solomon led a blameless life or did not experience failure or temptation. But by placing God at the centre of his life, he did gain peace, power and purpose.

Although most of us may occasionally hanker after the 'good life', seeking fame and fortune, material possessions will ultimately do little to prepare us to face the real issues of life and give us the strength and confidence to face trials, disappointments and temptations that, unless checked, will almost certainly lead to ruined relationships, a life that seems pointless and futile, and could lead to such despair that life itself seems no longer worth living.

Place your trust in God. Let him give you the power to influence those around you, let him give you inner peace and support when you need it and let him show you his purposes for you during your life on earth.

Prayer

We thank you for the varied society of mankind, into which we come, by which we are brought up and through which we discover your purpose for our lives. Guide us when we are in doubt or perplexed; and as we strive to be just and true, so may we constantly seek to order our lives according to your will.

Hymn

I'm not alone for my Father is with me
Songs of Fellowship, 235

Reflections

Talk

Light is needed to produce reflections. I am sure all of us spend a few minutes, or even longer for some, looking into mirrors every day. The reflections in a mirror are produced because light bounces from its surface to produce what is known as a virtual image. We are all familiar with the term virtual reality and the image in a mirror is a little like this. It is not a tangible thing, in that sense it is not real – it cannot be projected onto a screen like the image from a slide, which we describe as a real image.

The difference between a window and a mirror lies in the layer of silvered paint that has been placed on the glass in one case and not in the other. But the difference in perspectives produced is quite stark. In the case of the window you are able to observe what is happening beyond it, it gives you views beyond your immediate surroundings but the mirror is only able to focus on you.

Observations through windows on the world around us make us aware of other people and their lives, whereas the reflected image in a mirror is centred on self.

Our hearts and minds work in similar ways to the window and the mirror. We can either be inward or outward looking. Is your mind a mirror or a window? People can often be unhappy because they only focus on themselves, unhappiness overtakes you because you stop thinking of others, and you begin to think only of yourself.

The way people feel happy is by loving God and loving others more than themselves. No one is more miserable than a vain, self-centred person.

The window is made of glass, and the mirror is made of glass. But the glass of the mirror has been covered with silver. As soon as you add the silver, you cease to see others and instead see only yourself. Similarly closing our hearts and minds to the word of God closes the window to understanding the world around us and responding to the needs of others rather than just focusing on ourselves.

Prayer

Lord, let your light shine in our lives; help us to open our minds, so that we can see and act on the needs of others, rather than being blinded by our own reflections.

Hymn

Lord, the light of your love
The Source, 335; *Songs of Fellowship*, 362

Reading the score

Talk

When musical productions are staged, the musicians and singers make extensive use of the score for the musical. Without it, the musicians wouldn't know which notes to play or the singers what words to sing. The score is essential if the production is to succeed.

Of course, the score itself has an author, the person who first wrote and composed the words and music for the musical. Indeed, the success of the production depends as much on the performers as it does on the quality of the score and the person who wrote it.

The instructions in the score enable the various musicians and singers to harmonise to produce a meaningful and purposeful production. Even though there are different instruments and singers, through instructions in the score they are able to perform as one; in harmony and with a common purpose and function.

In many ways, the Bible is the score that unites us in life. The author, God, through his score is able to bring together the disparate people of the world and harmonise them with one accord, united in the belief that there is a purpose to life, that God is the creator of all, and that through faith in him we can be sure of eternal life once our temporal existence has ended.

But rather like the instrument player who plays their own tune, in their own time, there are people in the world who do not want to follow the score outlined in the Bible. They are not willing to contribute to the harmonisation process, preferring instead to think only of self.

Ultimately, the player who fails to follow the musical score will lose their right to be a member of the orchestra. Similarly, those who are unable to harmonise with others, who constantly ignore the instructions in God's score, will lose the right to life and freedom; either on earth or in the life to come.

How well are you following your part – are you improvising too much, or are you closely following the instructions of the master composer in his score?

Prayer

Lord, give each of us the wisdom to understand and apply your words as written in the Bible, and the humility to seek help from you when we need further instructions and interpretation in applying your score to our lives.

Hymn

Come, let us sing for joy to the Lord
Songs of Fellowship, 71

Reputations

Talk

One thing we know about reputation is that it is very hard to build up a good reputation, but very easy to lose one. We can all think of examples of this in public life – such as famous athletes who are found to have taken drugs and lose their medals and their reputations overnight.

People work hard to secure a fine reputation. As a school, we need to remember that our reputation depends on the way we all behave in the local community, pupils and teachers alike.

Throughout history, reputations have been lost and won – and reputations of those who have achieved success live on.

The outstanding achievements of individuals will always attract publicity and public recognition – and, usually, enhance reputation. Equally, in terms of how the local community will judge a school over time, it is often the everyday, unsung actions by pupils that matter most.

And we should always remember that the thoughtless actions of one or two members of a community can bring blame and criticism upon everyone else. We are as strong as the weakest link in our chain.

The following passage taken from Ecclesiastes reflects on those unsung members of the community.

The quiet words of the wise are more to be heeded
than the shouts of a ruler of fools.
Wisdom is better than weapons of war,
but one sinner destroys much good.

As dead flies give perfume a bad smell,
so a little folly outweighs wisdom and honour.
The heart of the wise inclines to the right,
but the heart of the fool to the left.

Even as he walks along the road,
the fool lacks sense
and shows everyone how stupid he is.
If a ruler's anger rises against you,
do not leave your post;
calmness can lay great errors to rest.

Ecclesiastes 9:17-18; 10:1-4

You don't have to be famous or infamous to have a reputation. The question we all need to consider is what reputation do we want to give our family, friends and the community.

Prayer

Father, forgive us for all our faults remembered and forgotten, for all the things we ought to have done and have not done, for the things we have done which have tarnished our reputation and brought sorrow to ourselves and others. Thank you for listening to our prayers and for sending Jesus Christ to forgive our sins and transgressions.

Hymn

Healing grace
Songs of Fellowship, 157

Resolutions

Talk

If you were like me last week, the start of the New Year, you will have made a list of New Year's resolutions. My list included:

- cutting down on chocolate biscuits;

- spending more time with the family;

- trying to do more exercise.

I have already failed with resolutions one and three.

Establishing New Year's resolutions is about reflecting on your lifestyle, the way you behave to others, thinking through priorities and trying to eliminate some of your weaknesses. Many people go through this yearly routine but research shows that for the majority of us it is a wasted exercise. Resolutions are soon forgotten as temptations come your way.

The year 2000 was very special since it signalled the end of the twentieth century. It gave us all the unique opportunity of celebrating the end of the millennium. It will be a thousand years before we are presented with the opportunity again. In fact it will be our great, great, great, great, great, great, great, great, great, great, great grandchildren who will be seeing in the year 3000.

We would not be celebrating AD 2000 if it had not been for the birth of Jesus Christ. The terms BC (before Christ) and AD (anno Domini – the year of the Lord) are only part of our modern language because of this one momentous and significant event 2000 years ago.

It is interesting to note that the ruling council of Jews at the time of Christ thought that Jesus would soon be forgotten and replaced by some other cult figure. In addressing the Sanhedrin (the ruling council of Israel) Gamaliel said the following:

Men of Israel, consider carefully what you intend to do to these men (the Apostles). Some time ago Theudas appeared, claiming to be somebody, about four hundred men rallied to him. He was killed, all his followers were dispersed, and it all came to nothing. After him, Judas the Galilean appeared in the days of the census and led a band of people in revolt. He too was killed, and all his followers were scattered. Therefore, in the present case I advise you: Leave these men alone! Let them go! For if their purpose or activity is of human origin, it will fail. But if it is from God, you will not stop these men; you will only find yourselves fighting against God.
Acts 5:35-39

So, I would suggest you ought to include the following two New Year's resolutions in your list:

- resolve to find out more about God by studying his word in the Bible;

- resolve to seek God's help and guidance by talking to him through prayer.

Prayer

Lord, help us in our resolve to seek and know you better and enable us to put into practice the teachings of Jesus Christ your Son. We pray for the generation to which we belong, those with whom we share a common fund of memory, common standards of behaviour and a common attitude towards the world.

Grant that the presence of Christ may be so real to us that we may be able to help our generation to see him also as our contemporary.

Hymn

I will seek your face, O Lord
The Source, 268; Songs of Fellowship, 276

Rights and responsibilities

When we start work most of us are given a contract of employment. This sets out our rights and responsibilities within the organisation, and generally gives an indication of the expectations the company have of our work. Reading between the lines, it also suggests the likely consequences if we fall short of the contractual obligations. To ensure that it is binding on both sides, the company and the employee normally sign the contractual document.

In Deuteronomy, Moses spells out to the Hebrews what it means having a contract with God Almighty. As part of the agreement, God promises that if the Hebrews keep his laws and commandments, he will defeat their enemies, assure good weather, a boom economy, health, prosperity and a country that will take the lead amongst all nations.

On the other hand, failure to keep to the contract agreement by disobeying God's commands will lead to wasting disease, with fever and inflammation, scorching heat and drought, blight and mildew and the country being defeated by its enemies and scattered to the four corners of the world.

More than anything God longed for the covenant with the Hebrews to succeed:

Oh, that their hearts would be inclined to fear me and keep all my commands always, so that it might go well with them and their children for ever! Deuteronomy 5:28-30

The rest is history. Israel and Judah did not keep their side of the bargain and as a result, about five hundred years before Christ's birth, were destroyed, except for a small remnant, by the Assyrians and Babylonians, who God had used to punish them for their obstinacy and disobedience.

Christ, however, heralded a new covenant (contract). The old covenant was the contract of law between God and Israel. The new contract is the covenant of grace, Christ's offer to forgive our sins and bring us to God through his sacrificial death. It is new in extent; it goes beyond Israel and Judah to include all Gentile nations. It is new in application, because it is written on our hearts and in our minds. It offers a new way to forgiveness, not through animal sacrifice but through faith.

Under God's new covenant, God's law is inside us. It is no longer an external set of rules and principles. The Holy Spirit reminds us of Christ's words, activates our consciences, influences our motives and desires, and makes us want to obey. Now doing God's will is something we desire with all our heart and mind provided we place our trust and faith in the risen Christ.

Have you entered into the new contract and begun walking in the better way?

Achieving a balance between people's rights and responsibilities – so that it is fair for all – needs everybody's co-operation and support. Remember that nobody is an island, separated from others, everybody is a piece of the continent, a part of the whole.

The Apostle Paul uses the concept of the human body to teach how Christians should live and work together. Just as the parts of the body function under direction of the brain, so Christians are to work together under the command and authority of Jesus Christ.

The body is a unit, though it is made up of many parts; and though all its parts are many, they form one body. So it is with Christ. For we were all baptised by one Spirit into one body and we were all given the one Spirit to drink.

If one part suffers, every part suffers with it; if one part is honoured, every part rejoices with it. 1 Corinthians 12:12-13, 26

Prayer

Lord, we are thankful for the individual talents you have given us. Help us share these with our friends, families and colleagues so that we can be brought nearer to you through servitude and praise.

Hymn

The King is among us, his Spirit is here
Songs of Fellowship, 532

Rubbish

Talk

What I am going to talk about this morning is a complete load of rubbish. Of course, there may be some of you who think that's all I talk about anyway, so what's new? Most people hoard rubbish – just take the contents of a lady's handbag, for example. Old lipsticks, the odd piece of chewing gum, out-of-date credit cards, empty nail varnish bottles and so on. Men fare no better as we hoard bits of wire, string, nails, parts of old TVs or radios and so on.

Children, especially the very young, are as bad. Just try throwing away torn comics, broken toys or dried-up felt-tip pens.

Twenty million tons of rubbish is cleared from our homes every year. It only takes one month to create our own weight in rubbish. What a mess! What trouble it causes when it's not collected by the bin-men and properly disposed of. Bags of decaying rubbish attract rats and create serious health hazards. We are very fortunate in this country to have regular and safe disposal of our rubbish.

But what about the rubbish in our spiritual lives? There is all sorts of rubbish there that needs safe and regular disposal too. For example our thoughtlessness, our unkind words, our unkind thoughts, our selfishness, our dishonesty, our greed and so on.

These parts of us are the sin, the rubbish we must make an effort to throw away. What we need is a big black bin sack to collect it all up and take it away. That's why regularly in our worship we have time of prayer asking God to forgive us the wrong we keep doing and help us to lead new lives.

Rubbish, though, keeps accumulating. It sneaks up on you like your household rubbish does. For instance, when you've had a good clear-out of the kitchen cupboards, the toy box or the garden shed, everything seems neat and tidy, but before long yet another clear-out is needed.

In the same way we need to regularly clear out the rubbish in our spiritual lives by asking God for forgiveness and new direction on a regular basis.

Prayer

Jesus, Son of God, we know that each one of us harbours sinful thoughts, words and deeds. Help us to turn from what is wrong in our spiritual life and to remove the rubbish it contains, so that we can come to you with purity of heart and mind.

Hymn

Draw me closer, Lord
The Source, 84; *Songs of Fellowship*, 81

Rules for living

If you think about it, our lives are controlled by rules and regulations. Some of these rules are enshrined in law, others are commonly agreed rules which allow us to live in an ordered and civilised way.

For example, the law that requires cars to be driven on the left in this country ensures we don't have chaos on our roads.

In classrooms, we have the simple rule of listening when being given instructions. It is not a criminal offence to break this rule, but in not following it, we would prevent others from learning and sanctions would need to be taken by the teacher to ensure compliance.

Christians believe that the fundamental laws concerning the way in which we should live are those handed down to Moses on Mount Sinai by God, known as the ten commandments.

The difficulties that society face today are because of the varying interpretations given to these primary laws. An updated version might read as follows:

1. Everyone's doing it, so why can't I?

2. It's the price of a free society.

3. There's nothing you can do about it.

4. You must move with the tide.

5. Who are you to talk?

6. You can't turn the clock back.

7. The problem is much more complex than you think.

8. You've got to look after number one.

9. It's never been any different.

10. It's all right so long as I don't hurt anyone.

The difficulty with this is that what other ages found offensive – crudity, incivility, obscenity, blasphemy and so on – are so commonplace today that they are almost routine.

At the same time, what other generations saw as essential to civilisation – moral codes, the capacity to differentiate right from wrong – has become not just controversial but taboo as we move into society dominated by the 'politically correct' movement. Merely to suggest that there may be some ways of life more gracious, honourable, decent, righteous and benign than others is to risk accusations of judgementalism, discrimination and moral panic.

The early Christians experienced great hardship and cruelty as they spelt out why people should follow God's commandments and the significance of Jesus' crucifixion. It was not because they wished to interfere in people's lives but because they knew life was short, and the penalty for wrong living will be long.

Time and again in the Bible there are examples of nations that have failed as their society spiralled into the decadent abyss created by not adhering to the word of God. The message given to Titus, a Greek, by Paul, is as apt today as it was then:

For the grace of God that brings salvation has appeared to all men. It teaches us to say 'No' to ungodliness and worldly passions, and to live self-controlled, upright and godly lives in this present age. Titus 2:11-12

Prayer

Lord, thank you for always being with us, especially when we are tempted to break your commandments. We pray that through your great mercy and exceptional grace, you will guide and lead us through our daily lives so that we can live self-controlled and upright lives in the name of Jesus Christ.

Hymn

Such love, such grace!
Songs of Fellowship, 515

Rules of the game

The whistle pierces the air, and all action on the field abruptly stops. Pointing to the player, the referee shouts, 'Foul!' and sends him off the field.

Rules, fouls and penalties are part of any game and are regulated and enforced rigorously by referees, umpires, judges, and other officials. Every participant knows that boundaries must be set and behaviour monitored, or the game will degenerate into chaos.

There are laws of the world as well – boundaries and rules for living established by God. But men and women regularly flaunt these regulations, hiding their infractions or overpowering others and declaring that makes it right. God calls this sin – wilful disobedience, rebellion against his control, or apathy. And at times the violators succeed – no whistle blows, no fouls are called, and individual dictators rule. The truth is, however, that ultimately justice will be served in the world. God will settle all accounts.

Solomon gives much advice about right living and following the laws of the world established by God. The following reading is taken from Proverbs in which he advises us that the law of God makes sense.

The wicked man flees though no one pursues,
  but the righteous are as bold as a lion.
When a country is rebellious, it has many rulers,
  but a man of understanding and knowledge maintains order.
A ruler who oppresses the poor is like a driving rain
  that leaves no crops.
Those who forsake the law praise the wicked,
  but those who keep the law resist them.
Evil men do not understand justice,
  but those who seek the Lord understand it fully.
Better a poor man whose walk is blameless
  than a rich man whose ways are perverse.
He who keeps the law is a discerning son,
  but a companion of gluttons disgraces his father.
He who increases his wealth by exorbitant interest
  amasses it for another, who will be kind to the poor.
If anyone turns a deaf ear to the law, even his prayers are detestable.
He who leads the upright along an evil path will fall into his own trap,
  but the blameless will receive a good inheritance.
A rich man may be wise in his own eyes,
  but a poor man who has discernment sees through him.

When the righteous triumph, there is great elation;
    but when the wicked rise to power, men go into hiding.
He who conceals his sins does not prosper,
    but whoever confesses and renounces them finds mercy.
Blessed is the man who always fears the Lord,
    but he who hardens his heart falls into trouble.
Like a roaring lion or a charging bear
    is a wicked man ruling over a helpless people.

A tyrannical ruler lacks judgement,
    but he who hates ill-gotten gain will enjoy a long life.
A man tormented by the guilt of murder will be a fugitive till death;
    let no one support him.
He whose walk is blameless is kept safe,
    but he whose ways are perverse will suddenly fall.
He who works his land will have abundant food,
    but the one who chases fantasies will have his fill of poverty.
A faithful man will be richly blessed,
    but one eager to get rich will not go unpunished.
To show partiality is not good –
    yet a man will do wrong for a piece of bread.
A stingy man is eager to get rich and is unaware that poverty awaits him.
He who rebukes a man will in the end
    gain more favour than he who has a flattering tongue.
He who robs his father or mother and says, 'It's not wrong' –
    he is partner to him who destroys.
A greedy man stirs up dissension,
    but he who trusts in the Lord will prosper.
He who trusts in himself is a fool,
    but he who walks in wisdom is kept safe.
He who gives to the poor will lack nothing,
    but he who closes his eyes to them receives many curses.
When the wicked rise to power, people go into hiding;
    but when the wicked perish, the righteous thrive.
Proverbs 28:1-28

Prayer

Lord, help us in our daily lives to live by those rules we know are right, give us the courage to resist temptation and to challenge those things we know are wrong.

Hymn

Breathe on me, Breath of God
The Source, 57; Songs of Fellowship, 51

Salt of the earth

Salt is a remarkable compound made from the ionic bonding of sodium and chlorine to make sodium chloride, common table salt.

It has many uses including the curing of meats, the seasoning of food, raising the boiling point of water, preserving foods, defrosting icy roads, killing slugs and as a mild antiseptic. The body cannot do without salt, but too much of it can also kill us. In ancient times salt was used as a method of paying wages, generations of mankind have always valued the properties of salt.

You are probably familiar with such phrases as, 'to rub salt into the wound' and 'salt of the earth', or the advice that if you spill salt you should take a pinch and throw it over your shoulder for good luck. Throughout history salt has played an important part in the daily lives of people.

Salt is referred to in a number of places in the Bible. It first appears in Leviticus where Moses writes:

Season all your grain offerings with salt. Do not leave the salt of the covenant of your God out of the grain offerings; add salt to all your offerings. Leviticus 2:13

In Arab countries, an agreement was sealed with a gift of salt to show the strength and permanence of the contract. The offerings were seasoned with salt as a reminder of the people's contract with God.

In Matthew's Gospel believers are referred to as the 'salt of the earth'.

You are the salt of the earth. But if the salt loses its saltiness, how can it be made salty again? It is no longer good for anything, except to be thrown out and trampled by men. Matthew 5:13

Salt is a good symbol of God's activity in a person's life, because it penetrates, preserves, and aids healing. Let the salt you use each day remind you that you are one of God's contracted people who actively helps preserve and purify the world.

If seasoning has no flavour, it has no value. If Christians make no effort to affect the world around them, they are of little value to God. Christians should affect others positively, just as seasoning brings out the best flavour in food.

Jesus used salt to illustrate the need to make a difference in the 'flavour' of the world we live in and to counteract the moral decay in society just as salt preserves food from decay. When we lose the desire to 'salt' the earth with the love and message of God, we have become useless to him.

Being 'salty' is not easy, but if a Christian fails in this function, he or she fails to represent Christ in the world.

How salty are you?

Prayer

Lord God our Father,
    we pledge ourselves to serve you and all mankind,
    in the course of justice and peace,
    for the relief of want and suffering,
    and for the praise of your Name.
Guide us by your spirit; give us wisdom;
    give us courage; give us hope;
    and keep us faithful now and always.

Hymn

Here I am, wholly available
The Source, 161; *Songs of Fellowship*, 167

Seeing the light

Talk

Light is an amazing thing – it travels at 300 million metres per second and can travel through a vacuum. It takes just eight minutes to reach us from the sun which is 93 million miles away. In the time taken to write this it could travel to the moon and back.

Have you ever wondered what it would be like living in a world without light. There would be no colours; no shadows to give perspective and objects would just blend into their background. But more significantly, without light there would be no food since the process of photosynthesis could not take place. Sure, we could use artificial light by generating electricity – but even that would eventually fail as the world's sources of fuel were used up. Indeed, it is interesting to note that coal, oil and gas are themselves just sources of light energy that were trapped by plants millions of years ago. To have light means to have life.

It is not surprising therefore, that John the apostle describes Jesus as the 'true light that gives light to every man' or why Jesus tells his disciples that they are the light to the world, meaning that the light of Jesus' truth is revealed to us, not hidden, and by allowing the light of truth into our lives we too will have life.

Sadly, some have not seen the light. In society we have those who bully, steal, lie, cheat and are only concerned with themselves, driven by selfish motives and greed. For them the light has been extinguished by temptations and the traps set by a materialistically driven society. But there is a ray of hope for all of us – the teaching of Jesus and the words in the Bible show it is never too late to change our ways. God is willing and wanting to forgive all those who confess their faults to him and turn away from the darkness of sin to the light of truth.

If a lamp doesn't help people see, it is useless. Does your life show other people how to find God and how to live for him? If not, ask what has extinguished your light. Complacency, resentment, stubbornness of heart, or disobedience can keep God's light from shining through you to others.

You are the light of the world. A city on a hill cannot be hidden. Neither do people light a lamp and put it under a bowl. Instead they put it on its stand, and it gives light to everyone in the house. In the same way, let your light shine before men, that they may see your good deeds and praise your Father in heaven. Matthew 5:14-16

Prayer   Father God, help us all to see the light of truth and become beacons for your word in the world in which we live.

Hymn   Light has dawned that ever shall blaze
Songs of Fellowship, 341

Servitude

Talk

A number of years ago there was a television series called *Upstairs-Downstairs* in which the daily lives of the maids, servants and the butler who lived downstairs were contrasted with those of the rich aristocracy who lived upstairs. Living downstairs meant a life of servitude to others. Although few homes employ servants these days, there are still many examples of people willing to serve others; for example, the men and women belonging to the armed forces, the millions of people who give freely of their time to serve in scouting, guiding and other volunteer organisations such as helpers in hospitals, nursing homes and charity organisations.

Maundy Thursday is the day before Good Friday. The word *maundy* is very interesting. It comes from the Latin word *mandatum* meaning command. Most people think about maundy in connection with money – this is because since 1689 the monarch has distributed specially minted coins to the poor on Maundy Thursday.

The custom was actually started in the fourteenth century by King Edward III, but he did not distribute money, he washed and kissed the feet of the poor. Even today, the clergy present at the ceremony carry linen towels on their shoulders to remind people of the original custom.

The custom in this country dates back 500 years. However, as the following Bible reading shows, the origins can be traced back to the last Passover feast Jesus had with his disciples. The following day, Good Friday, he was executed by crucifixion.

It was just before the Passover Feast. Jesus knew that the time had come for him to leave this world and go to the Father. Having loved his own who were in the world, he now showed them the full extent of his love.

The evening meal was being served, and the devil had already prompted Judas Iscariot, son of Simon, to betray Jesus. Jesus knew that the Father had put all things under his power, and that he had come from God and was returning to God; so he got up from the meal, took off his outer clothing, and wrapped a towel round his waist. After that, he poured water into a basin and began to wash his disciples' feet, drying them with the towel that was wrapped round him. John 13:1-5

Jesus was a model servant, and he showed his servant attitude to his disciples. Washing guests' feet was a job for a household servant to carry out when guests arrived. But Jesus wrapped a towel round his waist, as the lowliest slave would do, and washed and dried his disciples' feet. If even he, God in the flesh, is willing to serve, are you willing to follow Christ's example of serving? Whom can you serve today?

There is a special blessing for those who not only agree that humble service is Christ's way, but who also follow through and do it.

Prayer

Lord, we are grateful for the many talents you have given us, the opportunities for sharing these with others, particularly those less fortunate than ourselves. Give us the humility to offer ourselves in service to others.

Hymn

Meekness and majesty
The Source, 353; *Songs of Fellowship*, 390

Sharing your talents

There are many ways in which we can help others, for example:

- helping younger brothers/sisters with their homework

- helping grandparents with their gardening

- making time available to visit old people in the community

- cleaning your bedroom

and so on.

God has given each one of us particular talents and skills, but unfortunately, in today's society, we tend to forget that the gifts we have been given can be used to benefit others apart from just ourselves. In fact, one of the major pitfalls of modern society is the 'I' mentality which places greater importance on the acquisition of material things and power than in using the gifts from God for the benefit of others.

I want to read to you a letter from a young lady who is currently working in Romania with homeless and ill children. Philippa is a very talented person. She left school just over two years ago with three grade A's at A-level and the opportunity to go to Oxford. She has a particular talent for languages and is a committed Christian. For her Gap year, she decided to work in Romania, where she learnt the language and worked in an orphanage, dealing with young children abandoned by their parents because they were HIV positive.

She has just recently returned to Romania to continue this work. The letter which I am going to read illustrates a number of points:

1. Being a Christian is not easy.

2. Her strength comes from her faith in God.

3. She uses the teaching in the Bible to guide her actions.

4. She uses prayer as a means of communicating with God and for seeking help and reassurance.

5. She is using the gifts of language and compassion for the benefit of others.

Reading from Philippa's letter:

The last few weeks have been a serious struggle with the hospital. It's really hard, especially as these children take up all your time and the ones who really need your love don't get any. I feel tired and beat up, and have the scratches and bruises to prove!

A few days later I was reading Nehemiah and of how, when Nehemiah heard of the struggle of his people, he cried out to God and spent four months in prayer and fasting before doing anything. I really felt that this was what God was telling me to do regarding the hospital (but maybe not for four months!).

And then yesterday I think I got some answers. I had a meeting with a lady named Ana who heads up an organisation called 'Heart of a Child'. I think they are the group with which God would have me involved.

Not all of us will be called to use our talents in this way, but the sharing of those gifts with others is an essential component of God's plan for us.

Prayer

Loving Father, give us the wisdom to understand and know how you want us to use the gifts you have given us for the benefit of others. We ask that at this time you give missionaries and your servants of Christ the strength to persevere in the face of difficulties and to carry out the work you have directed them towards.

Hymn

Change my heart, O God, make it ever true
The Source, 68; *Songs of Fellowship*, 58

Should you get angry?

Talk

Some people believe that Christians should never get angry and yet anger is one of the most basic human emotions. Everyone gets angry and anger can manifest itself in a number of ways; for example, from open hostility and physical violence to the coldness of a silent stare.

At times, anger can produce inner turmoil, the body responds to these feelings with a hot sweat and flushed appearance. On the other hand, anger can be experienced as compliance on the outside while resentment and hostility run just beneath the surface.

Because anger is so common to human experience, and because it is such a threat to relationships, it's not surprising that the Bible has much to say about the dangers, roots, and taming of anger. What the Bible shows us is that anger is neither right nor wrong until there is a motive.

Anger can be productive and loving, just as it can be destructive and selfish. In most cases, the anger that moves a person to do harm to himself or others is selfish. The first explicit mention of anger in the Bible shows its potential to kill. The account of Cain and Abel shows an example of a man angrily protecting and providing for himself rather than placing himself under the direction of God.

Man's anger is far different from the anger of God that is good, constructive, and loving. God knows that anger is an important and necessary emotion for a healthy person living in a sinful world. Being honest about our anger, therefore, is something we cannot avoid. The Bible teaches us that we should be angry about how sin harms you and others, but to avoid selfish anger, the anger driven by greed, jealousy and lust. Selfish anger destroys the passion for life, displacing faith and love. As James writes in his Gospel:

What causes fights and quarrels among you? Don't they come from your desires that battle within you? You want something but don't get it. You kill and covet, but you cannot have what you want. You quarrel and fight. You do not have, because you do not ask God. When you ask, you do not receive, because you ask with wrong motives, that you may spend what you get on your pleasures. James 4:1-3

Anger, driven by the right motives is acceptable, but driven by selfish desires is destructive and contrary to God's desire for us to live in harmony and love, graciously accepting the gifts and talents given us to carry out his purposes for our life on earth.

Prayer

Father, we accept there are times when our actions are selfish, when we desire more than we need, and when we needlessly get angry. Help us to control our anger and ensure that we only become angry for the right reasons, instead of being driven by our selfish motives.

Hymn

May my life declare the honour of your name
Songs of Fellowship, 387

Soldiers of Christ

In the First World War, Lord Kitchener spearheaded a campaign to recruit soldiers to the army. The slogan he used was 'Your country needs you'. Belonging to the army involves service, hardship and risks. When you sign-up you agree to serve your country, and during war life is tough, full of hardships and dangerous.

Similarly, Christians are called by Christ to join his army. A spiritual battle is constantly going on all around us as God's kingdom is being extended and we are called to be a soldier in God's army.

In being soldiers of Christ we are being challenged to serve others and to live a lifestyle different from that of the world. We are challenged to look out for the interests of others, not just for ourselves. The Kingdom needs people who are willing to serve and just do the ordinary everyday tasks that will get the job done and will challenge those things that they know are not right.

A soldier's life involves hardship. He must, by definition, be someone willing to endure difficult conditions and hardships. We will experience many trials as a member of Christ's army. There is, of course, always the option of the easier life but God hasn't called us for an easier life. He has called us to be servants and soldiers, not to be superheroes or conformists.

Soldiering involves taking risks. Our society wants a risk-free environment but God wants us to take a risk, not to avoid them at all costs. He wants us to step out of our comfort zone and take risks for him. If we're soldiers, we're going to have to be willing to put up with hardships for the Lord's sake.

In his letter to the Philippians, Paul the apostle talks of service, hardship and risk-taking as a soldier of Christ. This is what he writes:

Do nothing out of selfish ambition or vain conceit, but in humility consider others better than yourselves. Each of you should look not only to your own interests, but also to the interests of others. Philippians 2:3-4

I think it necessary to send back to you my fellow soldier who was ill and almost died for the work of Christ, risking his life to make up for the help you could not give him. Based on Philippians 2:28-30

Are you ready to sign up to God's army and become a soldier of Christ?

Dear God, help us to be soldiers of Christ: willing to serve others, take risks in order to spread your word and thankful for the trials that test our faith in you.

Hymn

Soldiers of Christ, arise
Songs of Fellowship, 506

Strength and power

Periodically newspapers and magazines feature lists of the world's most powerful or richest people, the inference being that these are the people we should be looking towards to influence our lives. They are the trend-setters, the people with connections in the right places, those who influence government policies and strategies. They have made the big time.

Today I want to draw your attention to a person who was, and still is, extremely influential despite having lived nearly 2000 years ago. He was influential, but would almost certainly not have been featured in any of the 'top 100' lists of influential people. He certainly wasn't rich and he positively denied he was powerful. He wrote a lot about strength and weakness and gave a lot of thought to the subject of 'power'. He even went so far as to say that he delighted in his weaknesses and, most curious of all, he wrote these words about himself: 'when I am weak, then I am strong'.

This is a strange paradox; what did he mean by 'weak' and what did he mean by 'strong'? What do you understand by these words?

In his lifetime this person travelled hundreds of miles across land and sea to spread the word of the Gospel and he faced the sort of opposition and hardship that would have made most people give up – we can judge the extent of the hardships he faced from the following paragraph written by him:

Five times I received the forty lashes minus one. Three times I was beaten with rods, once I was stoned, three times I was shipwrecked, I spent a night and day in the open sea, I have been constantly on the move. I have been in danger from rivers, in danger from bandits, in danger in the city, in danger in the country, in danger at sea. I have laboured and toiled and have often gone without sleep; I have known hunger and thirst and have often gone without food. 2 Corinthians 11:24-27

After years of preaching and travelling, founding and guiding the new Christian churches, he spent the last three years of his life in prison and was finally executed by Nero the Roman Emperor.

Paul was strong. He lived an extraordinary life. But perhaps most important of all, his radical questioning of what we mean by 'strength' provides us with one of the most challenging and relevant messages for our lives today and, unlike the people in the newspaper lists, he will remain as influential as he was 2000 years ago.

Prayer Lord, thank you for the life of Paul the apostle. Help us to put his words into action in our lives.

Hymn For I'm building a people of power
The Source, 109; *Songs of Fellowship*, 111

Stealing

The eighth commandment says that 'You shall not steal' or, to put it another way, it is talking about the integrity of our pockets.

Literally translated the commandment means, do not take what is not yours and to which you have no legal right.

Stealing, though, has many different meanings. It could include: the use of false weights and measures; extortion; usury; misuse of an employer's time and property; depriving the poor of their rights; failure to repay debt when able to; borrowing, then failing to return what was borrowed; fraud or embezzlement; wasting someone else's possessions; general dishonesty in buying and selling; paying inadequate wages, or delaying payment; indifference to the use of parental property; failure to seek the owner of something we have found; taking unfair advantage of others and ignoring the needs of our parents when they require help.

We can steal from God, our family, our national or local government, our employer, other people and ourselves.

We can steal by stealth, omission, deceit, violence, neglect and by 'turning a blind eye'.

We can take money, respect, affection and time.

We now have a society where many people do not see it as wrong to steal unless it inflicts hardship on someone. It is OK if the victim is: rich, an insurance company, likely to steal themselves and can afford to lose it.

Christians are not free from the temptation to steal and there are many opportunities for them to do so. For example, failing to own up when charged the wrong price, evading paying a bus or train fare, forgetting to return something that has been borrowed, accepting praise and credit due to other people, failing to use money for the purpose it was given and stealing the reputation of others.

Seemingly 'small' issues are fundamental to our integrity in a world that accepts them as normal.

God gives us our material resources; in giving our lives to God, we become stewards of our possessions, not owners. Rather than simply 'not stealing' we have the opportunity to show an extreme of generosity in our lives. This means we will seek the good and well-being of others, show honesty in action, avoid condoning or encouraging the dubious practices of others, operating with justice in regard to another person's property or possessions, give generously to help others, recognise that privilege involves responsibility, and material possessions used improperly carry a spiritual health warning.

Far from depriving others, we should supply their needs. This applies not only to money and possessions but also to love, encouragement and time.

What we are will ultimately determine how we behave, and what we are needs to be marked out by the quality of integrity.

This does not mean we are superior, only that we are seeking to live according to God's instructions with the help of God's Spirit within us.

Prayer

Dear Lord and Father of mankind,
> forgive us for anything that we have done
> which we should not have done.
Forgive us for anything we could have done
> much better than we did.
Forgive us for wasting time,
> and for spending time on the wrong things.
Forgive us for everything for which we are sorry now.
Help us to follow your commandments with truth,
> integrity and righteousness.

Hymn

Dear Lord and Father of mankind
The Source, 79; Songs of Fellowship, 79

Swimming against the tide

In order to spawn and lay eggs young salmon have to leave the ocean and swim upstream through fast-flowing rivers. It is a difficult, tiring journey; a journey they have been genetically programmed to follow. In a similar way, our journey through life can be equally as challenging, especially when we go against the flow.

Recently, the Manic Street Preachers were performing at the Millennium Stadium in Cardiff. Some sixty thousand fans were packed into the stadium. You can imagine the difficulty that you would have trying to enter the stadium just as everyone was leaving.

It is sometimes difficult to stand out from the crowd. It needs real strength; sometimes we go with the 'flow' just to survive. But 'going against the flow' may have benefits – after all, it's possible that the crowd is wrong.

To a large extent all of us get our ideas of what everyone else does and thinks from the media – TV and magazines. However, this is actually a very limited picture of what people do and think – it only represents *this* part of the world at *this* moment in time.

'Everybody does it', or 'everybody says so', is not a very well-founded claim. But even if it were true that 'everybody does it', it's still not reasonable to think that you have to do it as well.

The fact that it's difficult not to do something doesn't mean you don't have a choice. For example, you are at a party where it seems as if everybody is drinking excessively. You have a choice:

• you can join in and get drunk;

• you can leave the party;

• you can stay at the party but not drink.

The first option is the easiest. You could do this without having to think at all. The other options require you to do some thinking, to make a decision, and then stick by that decision – no matter what other people say. But don't deceive yourself by thinking that there is no choice.

In Matthew's Gospel, Jesus is quoted as saying the following:

The gate to hell is wide and the road that leads to it is easy, and there are many who travel it. But the gate to life is narrow and the way that leads to it is hard, and there are few people who find it. Matthew 7:13-14

When it comes to making choices about right and wrong it isn't easy to go in the opposite direction to most other people, especially if you feel as if you are on your own in the choice you have made.

Think about the choices that face you and ask yourself whether there are any areas of your life where you are 'going with the flow' when really you want to go against it.

Prayer

We are the work of your hands, Lord.
You have made us and love us,
   all our life is your gift,
   all your power was in our creation,
   and you will go on giving us grace upon grace.
Make us receptive and open,
   and may we accept your kingdom,
   let us live in your peace,
   with you all the days of our lives.

Hymn

One shall tell another, and he shall tell his friend
The Source, 406; *Songs of Fellowship*, 439

Tasting the goods

Talk

Parents often encourage their very young children to try different foods, especially when weaning onto solids. Very often young children refuse to eat them, even though they have never tried them before. They have made a judgement not based on fact but on an irrational fear of the unknown.

In a similar way, pupils in school limit their horizons by deciding they are not going to like a particular subject or activity although they have never tried it before. As parents and teachers know, pupils can be quite stubborn and awkward in their refusal to try things out, giving all sorts of reasons as to why they will fail or not enjoy the activity.

Unfortunately this attitude causes many pupils to lose out on life's opportunities. In our adult lives, we often regret not having taken advantage of the opportunities available to us when we were young.

Autobiographies of well-known people in politics, science, medicine, engineering and other fields suggest they decided early in their career that they would take advantage of any opportunities that came their way – they were risk-takers, never afraid of trying out new ideas or learning new things. They were prepared to test the waters and taste what was available before either accepting or rejecting them. They generally embraced opportunities, turning them to their advantage.

In the same way, people often reject God out of hand before tasting what he has to offer them in their lives. King David wrote the following:

Taste and see that the Lord is good;
blessed is the man who takes refuge in him.
Fear the Lord, you his saints,
for those who fear him lack nothing.

Come, children, listen to me;
I will teach you the fear of the Lord.
Whoever loves life
and desires to see many good days,
keep your tongue from evil
and your lips from speaking lies.
Turn from evil and do good;
seek peace and pursue it.

A righteous man may have many troubles,
  but the Lord delivers him from them all;
  he protects all his bones,
  not one of them will be broken.
Psalm 34

'Taste and see' does not mean 'Check out God's credentials'; it is a warm invitation: 'Try this; I know you'll like it.' When we take the first step of obedience in following God, we cannot help discovering that he is good and kind. When we begin the Christian life, our knowledge of God is partial and incomplete. As we trust him daily, we experience how good he is.

Be like David, taste the good things that the Lord has to offer; don't limit your horizons by your lack of trust and faith in him.

Prayer Lord, we pray that you give us the courage to turn to you, the wisdom to understand your word, and the willingness to place our lives in your hands.

Hymn O taste and see that the Lord is good
The Source 2, 913; *Songs of Fellowship*, 447

The apple

Not only are apples good for you but they present some interesting questions.

The apple is a very versatile source of food, used extensively in cooking. For example, it can be used for apple pies, cider, apple drinks, pig food, apple strudel, chutney, or for just eating as it is.

It is thought that a falling apple fired the imagination of Sir Isaac Newton, resulting in his gravitational theory, which explains why things fall.

If you cut an apple in half, the core is exposed, and in the core are the pips or seeds of the fruit. Now these seeds have an amazing potential, you see they have the potential to produce an orchard. Each seed can produce a tree, which in turn produces its own apples and they in turn produce more trees, and so on. Over a period of time, maybe ten or twenty years, this one seed could be responsible for producing an orchard of apple trees.

The purpose of the seed is to become an apple tree and it is clear it has the potential to fulfil this purpose. It would be strange indeed if, on planting, the seed grew into a pear or orange tree.

There are two important questions which this then raises:

- Where did the first apple tree come from? Was it from a seed and if so, what produced the seed? If not, how did the tree get there in the first place?

- How was the apple seed given the potential to achieve its purpose?

These are fundamental questions. It seems inconceivable that it happened by chance. If you consider what the earth was like at the time of its formation – much of it was molten rock and lava – it is unlikely that by chance just the right ingredients came together to form an apple seed. And then there's the fact that it would also need the right conditions in which to grow and flourish.

When this is multiplied by the millions of other species of plants and animals that exist on the earth it all points to something rather more spectacular than chance and probability being the cause.

We are told in Genesis:

Then God said, 'Let the land produce vegetation: seed-bearing plants and trees on the land that bear fruit with seed in it, according to their various kinds.' And it was so. The land produced vegetation: plants bearing seed according to their kinds and trees bearing fruit with seed in it according to their kinds. Genesis 1:11-12

The answer to my questions is clear. God created the first apple tree, gave it the potential to bear fruit and the ability to reproduce itself.

In some ways, we are like the apple seed. We have the potential to achieve the purposes for which we were created. An apple seed can only produce another apple tree, but each of us has a different and unique purpose. Some may end up as famous football players, politicians, teachers, writers, actors, and so on. What is clear, though, is, like the apple our purpose has been predetermined and we have all been given the potential by God to achieve it.

Prayer

Father God, we thank you for your creation and for creating us with a purpose and giving us the potential to achieve it. Help us to understand what your purpose for us is by seeking your help through prayer and reading your word.

Hymn

For the beauty of the earth
Songs of Fellowship, 112

The good life

An advert for an expensive car ran for a long time urging readers to 'Pursue happiness in a car that can catch it!', whilst in another paper there was a full-page advert for a certain brandy, which said 'Taste the Good Life'. Looking at adverts on the television, in the papers or magazines seems to suggest that the good life has to do exclusively with weight loss, eating (paradoxically), hairstyling, entertainment, celebrities, fancy cars and that's about it.

The good life of advertisements is eating a chocolate bar on a sun-kissed beach in paradise. It's being twenty pounds lighter, or looking twenty years younger. It's what you wear, or what you have. It's the holiday of a lifetime, the feel of an expensive luxury car, or the sip of an exclusive brandy. It's owning a second home in the country. This 'good life' is a mix of pleasure seeking, escapism and materialism.

More money is currently spent on advertising than on education, so in terms of influence advertising executives are our primary educators. They are successful, and therefore highly paid, teachers. We trust their message – and we go out and buy their stuff.

So what happens when we cannot achieve the advertisers' dream, when the 'good life' according to the lie we are given doesn't materialise. We are led to jealousy and deceit, to lives aimlessly chasing unobtainable promises, depression and low self-esteem and at its extreme a life of crime and violence.

To the Christian, Jesus offers an alternative model of the 'good life'. The real good life – as demonstrated by Jesus – was one centred on love for one another and in trusting and serving God.

And do not set your heart on what you will eat or drink; do not worry about it. For the pagan world runs after all such things, and your Father knows that you need them. But seek his kingdom, and these things will be given you as well. Luke 12:28-30

Provide purses for yourselves that will not wear out, a treasure in heaven that will not be exhausted, where no thief comes near and no moth destroys. For where your treasure is, there your heart will be also'. Luke 12:32-34

Place your faith in Christ rather than the temporary illusions of the virtual world created by advertising giants; begin to live the real good life today.

Prayer Lord, help us to prioritise those aspects of our life that are important to you. Give us strength and encouragement to denounce the materialism that surrounds us in our daily lives and to stand firm for what is true and right, so that we too can find the 'good life' with you.

Hymn Lead us, heavenly Father, lead us
The Source, 311; *Songs of Fellowship*, 321

The greatest sacrifice

The greatest act of giving is the giving of one's life for the benefit of others. The two world wars of the twentieth century saw millions of men and women dying to defend the right for freedom of speech and beliefs. History is littered with the many men and women who have sacrificed their lives for their beliefs, to protect others or because they have refused to pay homage to dictators or oppressive regimes. In the world today there are still countries where freedom of speech and the right to hold differing political or religious faiths is crushed by oppressive regimes.

The death of Jesus on a cross two thousand years ago is not simply an event in history. Each person today has to decide how he or she is affected by his death and how they will respond to it.

One of the results of sin is to cut us off from God. It is our doing, not God's. Nothing evil can exist in his presence, any more than darkness can co-exist with light. This is why he seems distant and unreal, and not concerned with our frustrations and worries.

The trouble with many people is that they go on thinking they can bridge the gap by their own efforts, by their religious activities and good works, hoping they are doing enough to please God. But of course, they can never be sure they have ever done enough to earn God's approval and forgiveness.

Jesus' death on the cross tells us that God loves us, accepts us as we are and forgives our sins as we put our trust in him. Jesus bore the consequences of all human sin.

As is written in the New Testament

For Christ died for sins once and for all, a good man on behalf of sinners, in order to lead you to God.' 1 Peter 3:18

Forgiveness of our sins rests entirely on the finished work of Jesus on the cross.

Paul sums it up in these words:

Let us praise God for his glorious grace, for the free gift he gave us in his dear Son. For by the death of Christ we are set free, that is, our sins are forgiven. Ephesians 1:6

There are many ways of giving but the greatest gift to mankind occurred two thousand years ago when Christ died on the cross. It is because of this act that we were able to celebrate in the year 2000, his millennium.

Prayer

Gracious and holy Father,
   please give us:
   intellect to understand you,
   reason to discern you,
   diligence to seek you,
   wisdom to find you,
   a spirit to know you,
   a heart to meditate upon you,
   ears to hear you,
   eyes to see you,
   a tongue to proclaim you,
   a way of life pleasing to you,
   patience to wait for you
   and perseverance to look for you.
(Prayer of St Benedict)

Hymn

He was pierced for our transgressions
The Source, 169; *Songs of Fellowship,* 173

The manual for Life

Talk

Those of you who own a computer will know that when you bought it, it came with a detailed manual explaining how to use it and for offering solutions to problems when they arise.

Cars, videos, televisions, washing machines, fridges, hi-fi's and so on all come with their own instruction manuals. Similarly, doctors, nurses, dentists and others involved in the medical world have access to thousands of manuals to help them with the treatment and diagnosis of patients' ailments.

There is one instruction book different to all others – indeed, it is the most sold book in the world. But unlike all the other manuals, it addresses the important questions about life. For example: why we exist; why the universe was created; the purpose of our life on earth; who is God; how to communicate with God and what happens when we die. It also gives the ground rules for the way we should live and conduct our lives. It offers support, inspiration and hope in a world that emphasises materialism, power, greed and ambition at the expense of others.

The Bible took 1500 years to be completed, written by about forty people. Among them were kings, a prime minister, a doctor, a taxman, fishermen and a farmer. Most of the writers never met each other yet through the Bible runs an amazing unity and agreement. The reason for this is that God spoke to the Bible's writers and guided them to write down his words and instructions. They were inspired by the Holy Spirit.

God spoke to men who were in close touch with him. Paul summed it up by saying 'All scripture is inspired by God'. This is why the Bible is different from all other reference books. Through it God speaks to us today and on every page is his stamp of authorship and authority.

The Bible tells us what God is like and how we can know him. Without it we would know next to nothing about him. We would have no idea why we are here or where we are going. The Bible sheds light on every kind of problem. It speaks with certainty on life and death and eternity. It is our guidebook from earth to heaven. It is the instruction manual for Life.

Just as manufacturers will not guarantee their products if the instructions are not followed correctly, God's guarantee of eternal life will be broken if we do not follow his instructions for right living given through his words in the Bible.

Prayer

Father, give us the wisdom and understanding to put your words into action. Help us to follow your instructions; support and guide us when we are tempted away from the truth.

Hymn

God is working his purpose out
The Source, 128; *Songs of Fellowship*, 135

The tax collector

I was sorting out some papers the other day when I came across the very first pay slip I received as a teacher. Up until then I had held a variety of part-time jobs as a student ranging from ice-cream seller to working in a butcher's during my holidays. But it was this first pay slip that signalled to me I had entered the world of work, had a full-time job and was being paid a salary. This meant I was paid monthly in arrears and received a statement telling me how much I had earned and transferred to my bank account.

I vividly remember to this day the disappointment I felt on opening my pay slip. Although my salary was £450 a month a massive £110 had been taken in taxes. In my part-time jobs as a student, I had always had cash in hand and there was never any mention of taxes or other deductions. As you can imagine, it was a bit of a shock to realise I didn't have as much money available to spend as I thought I would have.

Of course, taxes are essential in order to pay for education, housing, social services and so on; but this didn't help ease my disappointment in losing so much from what was a relatively small salary thirty years ago.

Taxes have never been popular, especially those unjust taxes levied hundreds of years ago to pay for armies to fight abroad or for furnishing and building castles and mansions for the aristocracy.

Two thousand years ago, at the time of Jesus, Israel was an occupied territory, controlled and regulated by the Romans. The Romans appointed tax collectors to collect taxes from the citizens as well as merchants passing through the occupied territory. The money raised was used to pay for the lavish lifestyles and armies of the Roman Empire. Tax collectors were hated by fellow Jews partly because they were seen to be supporting the enemy but also because they tended to be corrupt, charging commission for themselves in addition to the taxes demanded by the Romans, generally overcharging and keeping the huge profits. Provided the Romans received taxes due they turned a blind eye to the corrupt practices of the tax collectors.

We can read in the Bible the account of one of these tax collectors – Matthew, who was responsible for writing the first Gospel of the New Testament.

This is Mark's account of Matthew's meeting with Jesus who was teaching in the area at the time:

As he walked along, he saw Matthew sitting at the tax collector's booth. 'Follow me,' Jesus told him, and Matthew got up and followed him.
Mark 2:14

More than any other disciple, Matthew had a clear idea of how much it would cost to follow Jesus, yet he did not hesitate for a moment. When he left his tax-collecting booth, he guaranteed himself unemployment and hardship. By giving himself to Christ he signalled a radical change in his lifestyle and a reassessment of his value system.

Like Matthew, Christians are prepared to give and commit their lives to Christ. They personally trust in him as their Saviour and Lord. Illness and physical pain, tragedies, accidents and death will come to Christians as to others, simply because they are human. They will suffer because of other people's greed and selfishness, because they are part of society and what they do affects others for good or bad.

A Christian who has given their life to Christ can face the world and all it throws at them, the future, even death itself, with total confidence – not in themselves and their own strength and wisdom, but in the almighty, all-knowing, all-loving God.

Prayer

Let us give thanks to God the Father of our Lord Jesus Christ for the great mercy that fills us with such hope and confidence to give him control of our lives.

Hymn

I want to walk with Jesus Christ
Songs of Fellowship, 261

The tongue

Talk

I wonder how many times you have hurt someone by using your tongue? In my younger days we used to chant 'Sticks and stones may break my bones, but words will never hurt me' in response to the name-calling of others. You know the sort of thing – those who wore glasses were called specky-four-eyes, those suffering from acne were called spotty, and so on. The truth of the matter was that name-calling did hurt the recipient, more often hurting them internally rather than externally.

Whilst as adults we might not go in for such name-calling, it is still possible to inflict deep psychological harm by the inappropriate choice of words. It is extremely easy to use cutting remarks, sarcasm, malicious gossip or lies in order to damage or undermine a person's reputation.

The Bible says that the tongue – the smallest part of us which plays such a powerful role in producing our words – is a bit like the rudder of a big ship; relatively small but very influential. Or, it is like a spark in a forest that can cause a huge fire.

When we put bits into the mouths of horses to make them obey us, we can turn the whole animal. Or take ships as an example. Although they are so large and are driven by strong winds, they are steered by a very small rudder wherever the pilot wants to go. Likewise the tongue is a small part of the body, but it makes great boasts. Consider what a great forest is set on fire by a small spark. The tongue also is a fire, a world of evil among the parts of the body. It corrupts the whole person, sets the whole course of his life on fire, and is itself set on fire by hell.

All kinds of animals, birds, reptiles and creatures of the sea are being tamed and have been tamed by man, but no man can tame the tongue. It is a restless evil, full of deadly poison.

With the tongue we praise our Lord and Father, and with it curse men, who have been made in God's likeness. Out of the same mouth come praise and cursing. My brothers, this should not be. Can both fresh water and salt water flow from the same spring? My brothers, can a fig-tree bear olives, or a grapevine bear figs? Neither can a salt spring produce fresh water. James 3:3-12

You can use your tongue to discourage or encourage others. It costs nothing to use our words to build someone else up – instead of ourselves.

If you have ever had any gossip spread about you, you'll know how hurtful it can be. The Bible has some particularly useful things to say about gossip in a book of wise sayings called 'The Book of Proverbs'. See if you can see the wisdom in these words:

- Anyone who spreads gossip is a fool.

- No one who gossips can be trusted.

- Gossip is spread by wicked people; they stir up trouble and break up friendships.

- Gossip is so tasty – how we love to swallow it.

- Without wood, a fire goes out; without gossip, quarrelling stops.

A group of people called the Quakers are renowned for not saying much at all. They ask themselves these three important questions before they speak:

- Is it true?

- Is it kind?

- Is it necessary?

Perhaps we too should set ourselves the challenge of asking these three questions before we speak.

Prayer

Father, help us to be effective listeners, slow to anger but swift to offer help. Enable us to use our tongues to encourage rather than discourage, and to think before we speak.

Hymn

Father, we love you
The Source, 103; *Songs of Fellowship*, 102

The uniqueness of man

Man is a unique creature; distinguished from other animals by his imaginative gifts. He makes plans, inventions, and new discoveries by putting different talents together. His discoveries become more subtle and penetrating as he learns to combine talents in more complex and intimate ways. Unlike other animals, he is not a figure of the landscape – he is a shaper of the landscape. Man advances by discovering the fullness of his own gifts and talents, and what he creates on the way are monuments to the stages of his understanding of nature and of self.

Why is man unique among the animal kingdom? Why has he been singled out in this way, above all other animals?

To discover why, we need to turn to the story of the creation. The Bible tells us that God created the heavens and the earth. Behind the complexity and beauty of the universe is a God who planned and made it all. We have been made in God's likeness. This does not mean God has a human body. It means that, like God, we are able to love and choose, to think and make rational decisions. We have a mind and a will. We have been made to have a special relationship with him – to know him and love him, to belong to him and be his children.

We have been made to care for the earth and all living creatures, to develop and use wisely its amazing resources.

We have been made with very great creative skills in music, art, science, medicine and engineering. It is in our very nature to invent and explore. Where we see all these skills being creatively used we see God at work, whether he is acknowledged or not. For he is not only the giver of life in all its variety and richness, he is the very source of life.

Reading from Genesis:

So God created man in his own image, in the image of God he created him; male and female he created them.

God blessed them and said to them, 'Be fruitful and increase in number; fill the earth and subdue it. Rule over the fish of the sea and the birds of the air and over every living creature that moves on the ground.'
Genesis 1:26

Thank you for the life you have given us. Guide us and all mankind in the way of your will. Give us courage; give us hope; and keep us faithful now and always.

Hymn

Holy, holy, holy, Lord God Almighty!
The Source, 176; *Songs of Fellowship*, 183

Thermostat or thermometer?

Talk

Thermometers and thermostats are two types of measuring instruments with different functions.

A thermometer is controlled by the surroundings. For example, the reading on it in a living room would be about 21°C, whereas in a fridge it would change to about 5°C. When placed in boiling water it would change to 100°C. In fact, wherever it is placed it is changed and controlled by its surroundings. We could say it is rather fickle, it goes with the prevailing climate.

On the other hand, a thermostat controls its environment. You can preset the thermostat in a fridge to 5°C and the temperature of the environment will be forced to that temperature. Or you can preset the thermostat in a cooker to 200°C and the inside of the oven will respond and change to that temperature.

Whilst the environment controls a thermometer, a thermostat controls the environment.

This raises the interesting question as to whether you behave like a thermometer or a thermostat. Have you got control of your life or is your life controlled by others? Do you blend in with the crowd or do you change the crowd; do you influence or are you influenced?

Jesus called on all Christians to be thermostats – to change the crowd, to stand up for what is right and to spell out the message of God. Although at the time of Christ there were no such things as thermostats, in his teachings Jesus used the term 'light' to communicate that we are agents for change in the world.

You are the light of the world. A city on a hill cannot be hidden. Neither do people light a lamp and put it under a bowl. Instead, they put it on its stand, and it gives light to everyone in the house. In the same way, let your light shine before men, that they may see your good deeds and praise your Father in heaven. Matthew 5, 14-16

Prayer

Lord, we pray that our trust in you can make us a change agent for the world. Give us the strength to challenge what is wrong and to stand out amongst the crowd as a witness to your goodness and love, and a testimony to your word.

Hymn

We are your people who are called by your name
Songs of Fellowship, 571

Time to choose

I was recently on a railway platform where there were two posters adjacent to each other. One was an advert for a recently published book that was about power, money, greed and lust. The other poster had the following quotation from the Bible on it: 'For the wages of sin is death but the gift of God is eternal life through Jesus Christ our Lord.'

They reminded me of the extremes of hope and despair we can experience on our journey through life and set my mind to likening our life to that of a train journey. On Platform 1 the destination was the eternal city, whilst Platform 2's destination was death and destruction. Once on each train, the doors are locked and we are on a one-way ticket to the final terminal of life.

Life is a one-way process, rather like entropy, going from order to chaos. At each station we visit in our life we have an opportunity to alight, take refreshment for renewal, even though our journey is in one direction only. Now if you imagine the trains from each platform running on parallel lines, there is also an opportunity to change trains at the stations as we reflect about our journeys so far, even though we can't go back to our starting point.

On route to the final destination there are detours and excursions, although we have a strict timetable to follow if we are not to be left behind on the station. And as the trains approach their final destinations there is one final opportunity to switch tracks; our ticket to destruction can be switched for a ticket to the eternal city. The only requirement being that our pass is stamped with the words 'Follower of Christ'.

Neither journey is trouble-free or without cost. Each can suffer from breakdowns and delays, but each is guaranteed to reach its final destination. The people on board tend to reflect the destination they are travelling to. In the one there is much jostling for position, much bickering and anger; in the other there is room for everyone and an overriding sense of calm and purpose. In the one there is concern about whether they will ever get there, about possessions that have been left behind; whereas in the other, people sit back and take in the view, seemingly unconcerned about the possessions they have left behind. In the one there is regret that it cannot go back to the starting point; in the other there is relief that places previously visited are left behind.

The contrast between the two journeys is stark, and the final destinations even starker. Have you collected your one-way ticket; do you know which platform to use; do you know where you are going; is your ticket correctly endorsed; is the final destination the one that you seek?

Trust in the Lord to show you the way to the correct platform so that at the final station you will not be disappointed.

Prayer Help us appreciate and value the gift of time you have given us, Father God. And, although the time we have on earth is a drop in the ocean, ensure that we put it to good effect both for the benefit of ourselves, and the benefit of others.

Hymn God is working his purpose out
The Source, 128; *Songs of Fellowship*, 135

Tragedy

All of you will have read or heard of the terrible train disaster near Paddington station in 1999 in which some forty people died. Since the accident, the papers have been examining the reasons for the crash, speculating whether it was due to signal failure, human error or a combination of both. For the families concerned it is a sad reminder of the frailty of life.

The following is an extract from one of the papers that reported not on the scene of the crash but on the commuter car park at Kemble Station, Gloucester.

As silent as tombstones, 19 frost-covered cars glinted in the early morning sun in the car park at Kemble station. I wonder how many cars in the car park aren't ever going to be driven again by the people who parked them yesterday. Among them were big, expensive cars – Land Rovers, Jaguars, BMW and a Mercedes. The silent witnesses in the car park at Kemble had their counterparts at stations across Gloucestershire yesterday morning. 'Empty, frost-covered cars that tell the tale', *The Times*, Thursday, 7 October 1999.

The article tells us much about the expectation that the drivers had of returning in the evening to their families and loved ones. All of us believe that we will be here tomorrow, that we are invincible. We make plans for the future and have an air of confidence about our life ahead.

The truth is that none of us can be certain of our future. As is so vividly portrayed in this report, lives can be taken without fore-warning and when we least expect it. The implication is that we must live each day according to God's will and be thankful for the opportunities he gives us each day we are alive.

Today many people are arrogant enough to think they don't need God. But our every breath depends on the spirit he has breathed into us. Not only do we depend on God for our very lives, he wants the best for us. We should also desire to learn more of his plans for us each day.

The train disaster is bound to raise in people's minds the ques-tion of why, if God is good, did he allow this to happen. God allows troubles to come because they:

1. humble us,

2. wean us from the temptations of the world and drive us back to God,

3. vitalise our prayers,

4. make us more dependent upon God,

5. encourage us to submit to God's purposes for our lives, and

6. make us more compassionate towards those in trouble.

We need not fear death because God is in control and has promised eternal life if we place our trust in him.

Prayer

Give us your Holy Spirit,
    to enlighten our minds,
    to see what we ought to do to strengthen our wills,
    to choose the right course of action, and abide by it;
    to empower our lives,
    to follow the right way to the end.

Hymn

I'm gonna thank the Lord, he set me free
Songs of Fellowship, 230

Triumphal entry

The hot-air balloonists that completed the circumnavigation of the world were given a hero's welcome in their hometowns. Similar scenes take place when famous people return in triumph to their hometowns. For example the winner of the Grand National, the FA Cup winners, an Olympic gold medallist, and so on. They normally attract large crowds of supporters and well-wishers who cheer and greet them on their triumphal procession.

On Palm Sunday, we recall another triumphal entry into a town – not the triumphal entry of a team, but of one man, a man who, although he hadn't won a trophy, was fulfilling prophecies made hundreds of years earlier, who on entering into the city knew that within a few days he would be executed on a cross and within seven days would have changed for ever our view of life and death.

Jesus Christ entered Jerusalem at the start of the Jewish Passover which was to celebrate the freeing of the Jews from captivity and slavery in Egypt thousands of years before. His timing was perfect since Jews from afar had journeyed to Jerusalem for the feast of the Passover, which meant there would be considerable numbers of witnesses to what was to take place. At the time, the Jewish nation were under occupation by the Romans and had been waiting for the promised Messiah or king who would lead them to freedom much the same way they had been waiting in Egypt to be led to freedom by Moses, thousands of years earlier.

There were many Jews who, despite having witnessed many miracles performed by Jesus, stubbornly refused to accept that Jesus was the Messiah, the son of God. This is illustrated by the account given in John's Gospel of the interrogation by the religious leaders of the day, the Pharisees, of the blind man whose sight was restored by Jesus.

They brought to the Pharisees the man who had been blind. Now the day on which Jesus had made the mud and opened the man's eyes was a Sabbath. Therefore the Pharisees also asked him how he had received his sight. 'He put mud on my eyes', the man replied, 'and I washed, and now I see.'

Some of the Pharisees said, 'This man is not from God, for he does not keep the Sabbath.'

But others asked, 'How can a sinner do such miraculous signs?' So they were divided.

Finally they turned again to the blind man, 'What have you to say about him? It was your eyes he opened.'

The man replied, 'He is a prophet.'

The Jews still did not believe that he had been blind and had received his sight until they sent for the man's parents. 'Is this your son?' they asked. 'Is this the one you say was born blind? How is it that now he can see?'

'We know he is our son,' the parents answered, 'and we know he was born blind. But how he can see now, or who opened his eyes, we don't know. Ask him. He is of age; he will speak for himself.' His parents said this because they were afraid of the Jews, for already the Jews had decided that anyone who acknowledged that Jesus was the Christ would be put out of the synagogue. That was why his parents said, 'He is of age; ask him.'

A second time they summoned the man who had been blind. 'Give glory to God,' they said. 'We know this man is a sinner.'

He replied, 'Whether he is a sinner or not, I don't know. One thing I do know. I was blind but now I see!'

Then they asked him, 'What did he do to you? How did he open your eyes?'

He answered, 'I have told you already and you did not listen. Why do you want to hear it again? Do you want to become his disciples, too?'

Then they hurled insults at him and said, 'You are this fellow's disciple! We are disciples of Moses! We know that God spoke to Moses, but as for this fellow, we don't even know where he comes from.'

The man answered, 'Now that is remarkable! You don't know where he comes from, yet he opened my eyes. We know that God does not listen to sinners. He listens to the godly man who does his will. Nobody has heard of opening the eyes of a man born blind. If this man were not from God, he could do nothing.'

To this they replied, 'You were steeped in sin at birth; how dare you lecture us!' And they threw him out. John 9:13-34

As we enter Easter week and re-examine the remarkable events of 2000 years ago we too should perhaps take stock and ask whether we are like the Pharisees, blinded by our own prejudices and arrogance, or like the blind man, prepared to open our eyes to the spiritual truths of God our creator.

Prayer

Lord Jesus, we are sorry it was necessary for you to die in such a cruel way on the cross. Help us understand the sacrifice you made for us and to remember with joy that death was not the end and that you rose again on the third day; our Saviour and our Friend for ever.

Hymn

My song is love unknown
The Source 2, 897; Songs of Fellowship, 400

173

Truth and its consequences

One of the phrases that most of us hear as we grow up is 'honesty is the best policy'. Whether it is our parents, our teachers or our peers, it seems that everyone is interested in knowing that they can trust what they hear us say.

Telling the truth is, indeed, very important. However, so many of us think that it is OK to be economical with the truth and then wonder why no one believes us any more.

But there is another aspect of honesty that we need to consider, living the truth. A popular book of several years ago asked this question in its title: 'Who are you when nobody is looking?' Are you one person in public, but another person entirely when you think you can get away with it. God calls for his people to be people of integrity, the same on the inside as they are on the outside. The Bible says, 'the Lord detests lying lips'.

Jesus had some choice words for the Pharisees who were trying to impress people with their outward appearance and behaviour but whose hearts were far from God.

The following is taken from Matthew's Gospel:

But do not do what they do, for they do not practise what they preach. They tie up heavy loads and put them on men's shoulders, but they themselves are not willing to lift a finger to move them. Everything they do is done for men to see. Woe to you, teachers of the law and Pharisees, you hypocrites. Matthew 23:1-5, 13

Becoming a Christian means being truthful and living for the truth. There are no shades of grey, no elastic boundaries. Lying to one another disrupts unity by destroying trust. It tears down relationships and may lead to serious conflict in families and between friends and colleagues. So don't exaggerate statistics, pass on rumours or gossip, or say things to build up your own image. Be committed to telling the truth, follow Christ's example.

Becoming a Christian means 'putting on a new self'. It means your conduct should match your faith; it means taking the right actions. This is a straightforward step that is as simple as putting on your clothes. Are you prepared to throw out the old and put on the new covering of Christianity?

Lord God, we come before you now to ask you to help us understand our duty – and to give us courage and self-control to stick to it, however hard we find it. We ask in the name of Christ our Lord.

Hymh   Be bold, be strong,
                The Source, 38; Songs of Fellowship, 37

TV – the false idol

The Simpsons is a popular television programme. Most can relate readily with Homer, Marge, Lisa, Bart and the baby Maggie Simpson. The fact that many of the situations portrayed are true to life makes the programme so appealing.

The opening scene in each episode follows the same pattern. The family are seen finishing work or school and rushing home to watch television. The communication between family members is minimal as they become mesmerised by the output from the screen.

I wonder how many of you do the same thing. Television is a wonderful appliance; and with the recent introduction of digital technology, the number of channels to choose from has increased dramatically. However, I am a little perturbed by this prospect, on two accounts.

Firstly, there are enough family squabbles already about what we should watch without having additional channels to choose from. Secondly, although television can be a source of entertainment and education, its method of communication is primarily one way.

There is already the danger that we know more about the lives of soap opera characters than we know about our relatives, next-door neighbours or our parents, brothers and sisters. For some, distinguishing between fact and reality is a real problem. It is not surprising that a few years ago the term 'couch potato' was coined to describe those who spent a disproportionate amount of their time watching television.

Although in biblical times there were clearly no televisions, it did not prevent God from warning us about the dangers of worshipping false idols. Television, like other human addictions, is one of our modern-day idols which, if we are not careful, can control our lives and hide from us the true purpose of life. Unless we remove idols from our lives, they can interfere with our faith and prevent us from the essential two-way communication with God. In Exodus we hear of God's anger towards those worshipping false idols:

'I have seen these people,' the Lord said to Moses, 'and they are a stiff-necked people. Now leave me alone so that my anger may burn against them and that I may destroy them.' Exodus 33:5-6

Have you any false idols which prevent you from communicating with God and keeping to your faith?

Prayer

Lord, we are surrounded by many temptations in our lives and it is so easy to consider them as more important than you, our creator. Help us to guard against false idols and give us the strength to resist their hold on our lives.

Hymn

Who is on the Lord's side?
The Source 2, 1066; *Songs of Fellowship*, 607

Twinkle, twinkle

Most of you will be familiar with the popular nursery rhyme 'Twinkle, twinkle little star'. The rhyme goes:

Twinkle, twinkle little star,
how I wonder what you are.
Up above the sky so bright,
like a diamond in the night.
Twinkle, twinkle little star,
how I wonder what you are.

Stars have always been a source of great interest. They have been used by countless generations of sailors as a navigational aid and this century astronomers have developed theories about how they are formed and learnt much about their life cycle. Our nearest star is the sun; without it, life on earth would be impossible. Physicists tell us that the source of energy in the sun is the nuclear reaction taking place in its core.

A great deal of this energy reaches us on the earth, providing our heating, lighting and the means for plants to produce the food essential for human survival.

If you observe the night sky you will see many thousands of stars and constellations. The ones we can see are just the tip of the iceberg since the number we cannot see is believed to number billions. It's something of a curiosity that we have night time at all, since with all the light arriving from billions of stars, space should surely be very bright indeed.

When we think of stars on the stage or in everyday situations, we usually visualise someone who stands out above the rest. The analogy with stars in the night sky is obvious, against a black background all stars stand out. Sometimes we don't see the stars because they are blocked out or outshone by others. Of course, you don't have to be a star on the stage to stand out. You can be a star in your classroom, in your family or in the community by standing up for those things which are important to you. You can be a shining example, a star.

In his letter to the Philippians, Paul the Apostle suggests that all Christians should be like shining stars, standing out above the rest. As stars Christians will be noticed, and therefore it is important that they live a life that is consistent with the teachings of Christ, beyond reproach and criticism; no cloud should be allowed to block out the light from the star.

Therefore, my friends, as you have always obeyed – not only in my presence, but now more in my absence – continue to work out your salvation with fear and trembling, for it is God who works in you to will and to act according to his good purpose.

Do everything without complaining or arguing, so that you may become blameless and pure, children of God without fault in a crooked and depraved generation, in which you shine like stars in the universe as you hold out the word of life – in order that I may boast on the day of Christ that I did not run or labour for nothing. But even if I am being poured out like a drink offering on the sacrifice and service coming from your faith, I am glad and rejoice with all of you. So you too should be glad and rejoice with me. Philippians 2:12-18

Prayer

Lord, help us all to be that shining light which reflects all that is good and consistent with your teachings. Help us to be true and never to forget that we must help other people before ourselves. Give us loving hearts and busy hands, so that we may know the joy of making other people happy. We ask this in the name of your Son, Jesus Christ.

Hymn

Lord make me an instrument, an instrument of worship
Songs of Fellowship, 360

Valuing others

Jesus tells the story in the Bible of the 'Good Samaritan'. It is a story about a man travelling from Jerusalem to Jericho. On the journey, he is robbed and left by the roadside to die.

Over the next few hours, three other travellers come across the man lying injured on the ground. The first, a priest, decided it was safer to cross the road and travel on the other side so that he didn't have to respond to the plight of the injured man.

The second person to arrive on the scene was a temple helper. He too ignored the injured man and continued on his way.

The third and final man on the scene was a Samaritan from Samaria. This was a country of mixed race between Jews and Gentiles, despised by the Jews. When he saw the injured man, he felt sorry for him, assisted him and took him to the nearest inn where he instructed the innkeeper to look after the man until his return. He agreed to pay the costs of looking after the man.

The point of the story by Jesus was to illustrate what he meant by loving your neighbour and understanding whom our real neighbours were.

He was saying that we each have a responsibility to help those less fortunate than ourselves. We don't have to be rich or special, because the gift of love is free to us all.

John tells us in his Gospel that love comes from God and anyone who doesn't love others has never known God. The priest and temple helper, whilst being experts in religious ceremony and Jewish law were short on love and compassion. John writes:

If we love each other, God lives in us, and love is truly in our hearts.
1 John 4:12

and

We know what love is because Jesus gave his life for us. That's why we must give our lives for each other. 1 John 3:16

In a secular society that promotes self at the expense of others, the challenge for all of us is to make that conscious effort to seek out those who need our love and offer it unconditionally as the Samaritan did for the traveller, and Jesus did for us. Have you made that commitment?

Prayer

Thank you, heavenly Father,
for making us as we are;
for hands to work and feet to walk and run;
for eyes to see, and ears to hear;
for minds to think, and for hearts to love;
for all the people we know, and who know us.
Help us to work together, supporting one another,
so that we are able to use in the most effective way
the talents you have given us.

Hymn

We are the hands of God, our task to do his will
Songs of Fellowship, 570

Visions

Talk

Certain individuals in history have had the ability to lead and inspire others in pursuit of an ideal about which they felt passionately. One such person was Dr Martin Luther King who felt he would not rest until justice and equal rights for black people had been achieved in the United States of America.

In August 1963 he delivered his famous speech, 'I have a dream', in which he outlined his vision for equality of opportunity and freedom of speech for all.

Does God have a vision for you? God still wants his people to be united and trained to do his work. As we recognise the deep needs in our world, God can give us the vision and desire to reform. With that vision, we can mobilise others to pray and put together an action plan.

What is God's vision for you? Are you ready to take on the challenge; are you open to receiving the vision; are you prepared to put God's principles before self; are you prepared to make the ultimate sacrifice to fulfil his vision for you?

Find out what that vision is for you by reading God's word in the Bible and seeking help and support through daily prayer. Do as the great prophets did, and act on the vision you receive by carrying out the action plan that God has tailor-made for you.

Prayer

Give us, O Lord,
   a steadfast heart,
   which no unworthy thought can drag downwards;
   an unconquered heart,
   which no tribulation can wear out;
   an upright heart,
   which no unworthy purpose can tempt aside.
Give us, O Lord,
   understanding to know you,
   diligence to seek you,
   wisdom to find you,
   and faithfulness
   that may embrace you,
   through Jesus Christ our Lord.
St Thomas Aquinas (1225-74)

Hymn

Be thou my vision
The Source, 50; Songs of Fellowship, 42

Water for life

Each year we hear of floods in different countries through the world and how they affect the lives of many thousands of people, causing untold damage and misery.

All living things need water. Many living things are made mostly of water: a tomato is 95 per cent water, a potato is 80 per cent water, an elephant is 70 per cent water, and we are 66 per cent water. Seventy per cent of the earth's surface is covered by water. Some of this evaporates and comes back down as rain. This rain fills up the seas, the rivers and lakes.

However, although there is a lot of water on earth, only 1 per cent is suitable for humans to drink. Ninety-seven per cent of our water is salty seawater and 2 per cent is ice. We should be grateful that we only have to turn a tap and we can drink; in some countries people have to walk up to 20 miles every day to collect water.

In this country each person uses about 5 litres of water for cooking and drinking every day. Having a bath uses 300 litres of water. Cleaning teeth and washing uses 30 litres. Washing-up uses 10 litres. Each toilet flush uses 13 litres. It takes 10 litres of water to cook 1 kilogram of rice. It takes 45 litres of water to make 1 litre of beer.

Each of us in Britain uses about 150 litres of water a day. In poor countries, a person only uses about 12 litres of water a day. Every year in India alone 20,000 babies die because they drink dirty water. Every day in poor countries 30,000 adults die because they drink dirty water. Over half the people in the world do not have enough water. Water is used many times in the Bible as a symbol of life. In the Old Testament, God promised his people good harvests. He promised to send rain to make the food grow.

He said, if you obey my rules and do what I ask you to do, then I will send you all the rain you need, just at the right time to make things grow. All the crops will grow beautifully in the soil and the trees will be covered with fruit. You will be able to harvest your food all the year round and eat as much as you want. Leviticus 26:3-5

Early men knew that they could not live without the water God sent to them. In the New Testament, water is still used as a symbol of life. When John the Baptist baptised Jesus, he used water to show that Jesus was starting a new stage in his life. When we are baptised, water is used to show that we are being given the power to grow for God. Jesus said that anyone who asked would receive living water and eternal life.

Prayer

We thank you, Lord Father, for water which keeps alive people, plants and animals; for water which keeps us healthy; for water to nourish our crops; for water which gives us new life in baptism.

Hymn

Eternal God, we come to you
Songs of Fellowship, 85

Waiting

Wherever you go these days almost everyone is in some state of waiting. At lunchtime you wait in line for your meal, in the doctor's surgery, there is always a queue, the checkouts at the supermarket are always fully occupied and the traffic lights seem to stay on red for ever.

Have you noticed, though, how different types of waiting produce different types of emotions in us? For one person, waiting is a positive experience, for another, a negative experience.

For example, if you are waiting for your brother or sister to finish in the bathroom because you want to get ready to go out, you are likely to experience frustration, even anger, the longer you have to wait. Conversely, you are unlikely to complain about waiting at the cinema to watch a popular film.

When happy anticipation is eclipsed by irksome frustration, waiting becomes anxiety-ridden and a negative experience.

Similarly, we are often frustrated in waiting for answers to our prayers, our waiting becomes a negative experience. It is assumed that if we present in our prayers all the areas of concern in our lives to God, he will immediately grant us our requests. This is not so, and the Bible is full of examples where people have become frustrated by this apparent delay in answering prayer.

David writes in Psalms:

How long must I have sorrow in my heart? Psalm 13

Why have you forgotten me? Psalm 42

The theme is repeated by others:

How long, O Lord, must I call for help, but you do not listen?
Habakkuk 1:2

Again and again, Habakkuk's word is punctuated with this complaint against God's slowness.

Too often we are like impatient children, rather than following Paul's advice:

Do not be anxious about anything, but in everything, by prayer and petition, with thanksgiving, present your requests to God. And the peace of God, which transcends all understanding, will guard your hearts and minds in Christ Jesus. Philippians 4:6-7

and

We know that in all things God works for the good of those who love him, who have been called according to his purpose. Romans 8:28

The significance of what Paul is saying is that if we have faith and trust in the fact that God has planned our life for us then there is no point in worrying or expecting instant responses. God determines the timing, and for those who trust in him, this timing will be the perfect solution to our petitions and requests, not when we perceive this should be, but when God knows according to the life plan he has mapped out for us.

Prayer

Loving Father, help us to place our trust in you to determine the timings for your intervention on our behalf. Help us develop patience and humility in waiting for your response.

Hymn

What a friend we have in Jesus, all our sins and griefs to bear! *The Source*, 566; *Songs of Fellowship*, 593

What goes wrong?

Nearly everybody loves babies with their appealing smiles and the funny gurgling noises they make. But have you ever noticed that babies very quickly take advantage of the situation, they soon take control? You see, like many of us, they are very self-centred, they want their own way and most of the time get it.

As toddlers, they have become quite adept at getting their own way. Witness the screaming tantrums in the middle of the supermarket aisle as a toddler, determined to get their own way, uses a not too subtle method of achieving it.

By the time they are teenagers they have amassed an arsenal of methods for satisfying their own self-centred lives. There is the well-tried sulking technique, used to good effect by generations of teenagers. Then there is the outrageous dress phase, where the sheer embarrassment of being seen in the presence of their son/daughter, causes parents to acquiesce to every whim and demand. Then there is good old-fashioned bribery and corruption. Teenager will do X if, and only if, Mum/Dad agrees to said conditions, which are generally weighted in the teenager's favour.

Adults are no better, although the methods they use become increasingly more sophisticated, often playing on people's insecurity and deep-seated emotions. We are all vulnerable to emotional blackmail and manipulation.

So, what has gone wrong as we grow from that loving baby to that ruthless self-centred adult?

This is all because God, who created a perfect universe, gave us the precious gift of free will. He did not make us like robots or machines. The gift of free will means that men and women can choose between right and wrong, good and bad. They can choose to love each other or not. You can choose to love God or not, to do what he wants or what you want, to live for God or for yourselves.

Sadly, many have chosen to ignore God's commands and laws for right living. This has produced a world that sees mindless deaths, corrupt governments, and dishonesty at all levels of society and the disregard of others in the pursuit of the selfish needs of self-centred individuals. The gift of free will has opened up the door for all kinds of wickedness which is undermining the very fabric of the society and world in which we live.

At first, sin seems to offer freedom. But the liberty to do anything we want gradually becomes a desire to do everything. Then we become captive to sin, bound by its 'yoke'. There is, however, a solution.

Freedom from sin's captivity comes only from God. He gives us freedom not to do anything we want but to do what he knows is best for us. Strangely, true freedom comes in obeying God, following his guidance so that we can receive his best.

My sins have been bound into a yoke;
    by his hands they are woven together.
They have come upon my neck
    and the Lord has sapped my strength.
He has handed me over
    to those I cannot withstand.
Lamentations 1:14

The free will gift is not without conditions. With it comes the responsibility to live within God's rules. Misuse results in death and destruction; responsible use guarantees a life of freedom and purpose.

Prayer

God our Father, we know that we have sinned against you in our thoughts, words and deeds. There are so many things we have not done which we should have done. Please forgive us and help us in the future not to be so self-centred, but to think more often about the needs of others.

Hymn

I am not ashamed to belong to Jesus
Songs of Fellowship, 199

What is the purpose of pain?

Talk

None of us like pain, or being witnesses to pain, although paradoxically we often inflict pain on others. One of the most common objections iterated by non-Christians is that if God is a good and loving Father, why does he allow pain to permeate the world in which we live? It is a difficult question to answer, particularly as Christians themselves often suffer considerable pain in their lives, although being a Christian should not make them exempt from suffering. Pain can be both physical and mental; who has not experienced the pain of losing a loved one, or watched hopelessly someone close to them suffering with cancer, or the pain of failure and rejection? Pain and suffering forms the backcloth to all our lives.

It is just as important to answer the question about pain as it is to understand how we should respond to it. The freedom to choose is at the heart of what it means to be human, and a world without choice would be worse than a world without pain. Neither would it be right for people who make wrong choices not to experience pain and suffering. No one is more dangerous than the liar, thief, or killer who doesn't feel the pain they are causing to themselves or others.

Without pain, the sick wouldn't seek a remedy, criminals wouldn't fear the law, and youngsters would sneer at correction. The examples of Solomon and David, lured by pleasure and taught by their pain, show us that even the humblest can drift from good and God until arrested by the resulting pain of their own imperfect choices.

The power for love, forgiveness, anger, jealousy and pride can lie unproven until awakened by pain. Strength of character is not found when everything is going well but when suffering and pain are present in our lives. As gold and silver are refined by fire, and as coal needs time and pressure to become a diamond, the human heart is revealed and developed by enduring the pressure and stress of time and circumstances. Strength of character is not shown when all is well with our world but in the presence of human pain and suffering.

The physical and mental pain experienced by Job is probably far greater than any of us will ever experience. But Job was left to conclude that if God had the power and wisdom to create the physical universe, there was no reason to doubt and trust that same God in our times of suffering and pain.

In this you greatly rejoice, though now for a little while you may have had to suffer grief in all kinds of trials. These have come so that your faith – of greater worth than gold, which perishes even though refined by fire – may be proved genuine and may result in praise, glory and honour when Jesus Christ is revealed. 1 Peter 1:6-7

Prayer

Lord, give us the courage and strength to live by your principles, the wisdom to discern right from wrong, and to seek your guidance at all times.

Hymn

Rock of ages, cleft for me
The Source 2, 951; *Songs of Fellowship*, 488

What you see is what you get

The Ford Motor Company once made the historic offer, 'You can have any colour so long as it is black.' Those days are long gone. Almost every make of car offers at least four engine sizes, twelve paint colours, three interior styles and further options on wheel trims, stereo systems, gearbox, electric windows, sunroof, and so on.

As a child, our family holiday was Blackpool or Blackpool. Recently I have been looking at places to stay this summer, weighing up the competing merits of seventeen different brochures.

When my parents first had a telephone they only had one decision to make – do we have it or don't we? There was no choice about where it should go – all telephones went in the hall. Today there are hundreds of different options available.

The scale of choice and the rate at which it is increasing bears no comparison to the world even twenty years ago.

In the mid-1970s the average supermarket offered some 9000 items, by 1985 this had risen to about 22,000, today it is probably nearer 50,000. Research shows that in a year we watch more than 9000 adverts.

Our subconscious is left to work overtime to cope with the insurmountable gap between what we desire and what we have – and how the gulf can be bridged. The problem of over-choice is not limited to our material consumerism. There are almost 3000 different Christian societies and organisations in the UK.

The difficulty with this over-choice is that it can, if allowed to, put each of us under considerable stress and pressure. We live in a society where instant solutions are demanded, where the only rest we seem to get is while the traffic lights are on red!

David, who wrote most of the Psalms, places things in perspective by knowing how trusting in God can release our tensions in time of stress.

My soul finds rest in God alone;
  my salvation comes from him.
He alone is my rock and my salvation;
  he is my fortress, I shall never be shaken.

Trust in him at all times, O people;
  pour out your hearts to him,
  for God is our refuge. Psalm 62

Trusting God to be our rock, salvation, and fortress will change our entire outlook on life. No longer need we be slaves to the stress created by over-choice. When we are resting in God's strength, nothing can shake us – what you see is what you get.

Prayer Father God, let us not forget in the rapidly changing world in which we live you are always there to guide and protect us.

Hymn Our confidence is in the Lord
The Source, 417; *Songs of Fellowship*, 452

Yeast for thought

There is nothing quite like the smell of freshly baked bread to get your gastric juices running. If you notice in supermarkets the bakery is placed at the furthest point from the entrance – the smell is guaranteed to make you walk through the store to the bakery. On the way, there you might just also pick up some of those tempting offers deliberately placed in your way.

The yeast put into the dough gives cooked bread its distinctive smell. These single-celled organisms are activated during the kneading and rising process to produce maltose and alcohol. They multiply very rapidly and cause the dough to rise, growing often two or three times its original size. The yeast cells are more active when it is warm, although above a certain temperature they die. The yeast permeates the whole of the dough, giving it its light texture.

The number of yeast cells grows exponentially with time. This means that its growth rate is very rapid, doubling the number every 20 minutes or so. It is because of this very rapid growth that only a small amount is needed to cause the whole of the dough to be affected by it.

In Biblical times yeast played an important role in the dietary requirements of people since bread formed a staple part of the diet, and there are two places in the Bible where yeast is used to illustrate rapid growth. One is in Leviticus where it is used to illustrate how sin can grow in our life and the other in Matthew as a symbol of kingdom growth.

The analogy in Leviticus makes the connection between a small amount of yeast needed to affect the whole loaf, the same as a little sin can ruin a whole life. In Matthew the parable of the yeast is recalled, which is:

The kingdom of heaven is like yeast that a woman took and mixed into a large amount of flour until it worked all through the dough.
Matthew 13:33

Although yeast looks like a minor ingredient, it permeates the whole loaf. Although the kingdom began small and was nearly invisible, it would soon grow and have an impact on the world.

Two thousand years later we can see evidence of that growth – are you part of it, or has the yeast yet to do its work in you?

Prayer

Thank you, Lord, for your words in the Bible; through your help let them permeate and multiply in our daily lives so we are brought safely to your kingdom.

Hymn   Break thou the Bread of Life
Songs of Fellowship, 50

Hymn   Break thou the Bread of Life
Songs of Fellowship, 50

You are what you believe

I wonder how many of you hold superstitions?

Friday 13th is one example of something which is thought to be unlucky. There are plenty of other superstitions – which people believe bring them bad luck or good – which may affect their lives in some way. For example:

- finding a four-leaf clover is supposed to bring good luck;

- throwing salt over your shoulder when cooking or eating. This is meant to scare off the devil who may have been following you;

- saying 'God bless you!' when someone sneezes. This was once thought to ward off any evil spirits you may have breathed in;

- saying 'Touch wood' or 'Fingers crossed'. Both of these sayings probably originate in the idea of trusting in the cross that Jesus died on;

- black cats were probably thought to be unlucky because of their association with witches;

- seven years' bad luck when you break a mirror. There were probably economic reasons for this superstition. The backs of mirrors used to be silvered with real silver and it would take seven years to save up the money to pay for it;

- don't pass on the stairs; don't put your shoes on the table; don't open an umbrella inside the house; and if you pull your face it will stay like that if the wind changes are further examples of superstitions.

The question is whether any of these superstitions are really worth believing or trusting in. In fact, they are really just a mixture of superstition, common sense, old wives' tales, economics, pagan and Christian beliefs. Put them all together and you have something which could be called 'folk religion'. Superstitions don't really have any power to bring you good or bad luck.

Many people today, even though they wouldn't call themselves religious, try to make sense of life and find security by 'believing' in some of these superstitions. To do this means – as in the major religions – they have to exercise a certain amount of faith.

In this country many people are turning their back on materialism and turning to New Age religions including the occult, horoscopes, faith in crystals or tarot cards.

Everyone believes in something but the challenge for you is to ask yourselves what you believe and what you are basing your lives on. What you believe affects the way you treat yourself, treat others and view the world, the universe and beyond. What you believe shapes your hopes and dreams for the future. So, it's important that what you believe in is true and worthwhile.

You are what you believe.

Prayer

O Lord, our Saviour,
who hast warned us that thou wilt require much
of those to whom much is given,
grant that we, whose lot is cast in so goodly a heritage,
may strive together the more abundantly by prayer,
by almsgiving, by fasting,
and by every other appointed means,
to extend to others what we so richly enjoy;
and as we have entered into labour of other men,
so to labour that in their turn other men may enter into ours,
to the fulfilment of thy holy will,
and our own everlasting salvation; through Jesus Christ our Lord.
St Augustine (354-430)

Hymn

This is the day
The Source, 517; Songs of Fellowship, 553

You can make a difference

In 1946, the first Tacoma Narrows Bridge collapsed in a steady, relatively light, crosswind. Although the wind was not particularly strong, it caused the bridge to start oscillating, and as the wind continued to blow, the amplitude of the oscillations grew, until eventually the additional stress in the structure became so great that it collapsed. The effect is well known in physics as resonance.

When pushing a child on a swing, the height of the swing can be increased by pushing just at the right time. This is another example of resonance. Although only a little energy is used for each push, the overall effect is to increase the amplitude of the swing substantially over a short period. In the case of the Tacoma Bridge, although the wind speed was relatively low, the effect was enormous, resulting in the collapse of the bridge.

Many Christians are under a misapprehension that they don't matter, that being a small voice in a largely secular world, they are unable to make an impact on the lives of people they meet. Consequently, in the workplace, at school, or in their own neighbourhoods, they tend to keep their Christianity to themselves. Firstly, because they are wary of imposing their beliefs on others and, secondly, they are not convinced they can make a difference.

If the early Christians had responded in a similar way, we would not have heard of Christ or Christianity today. Remember, immediately following Christ's death and resurrection, the world was an extremely hostile and violent place for the fledgling Christians. But energised by the Holy Spirit and a deep commitment to serve, they professed their faith and gave the world the truth and the light.

Although they were relatively small in number, the impact can be measured by the millions and millions of believers throughout the world today. Rather like the Tacoma Bridge, and the swinging of the child, their input, however small on a universal scale, produced a resonance throughout the world.

The message is clear; we do matter, we can impact, and we are an essential driving force for setting the world into resonance with the wonderful word of God, the promise of eternal life, the forgiveness of sins, and hope for humanity. However, like a resonating system, the oscillations can be damped, causing it to lose its energy and eventually decay to nothing. As Christians, we need to reduce the damping effects of political correctness, temptations, lack of courage and lethargy to a minimum, so that resonance can occur, and allow the world to resonate with praise and glory to God our maker and redeemer.

Therefore, my dear brothers, stand firm. Let nothing move you. Always give yourself fully to the work of the Lord, because you know that your labour in the Lord is not in vain. 1 Corinthians 15:58

Prayer

Loving Father God, give us the courage to act and intervene on behalf of others so that we can be instrumental in bringing them to know you and the hope and salvation you can give them in their lives.

Hymn

Our confidence is in the Lord
The Source, 417; Songs of Fellowship, 452

Index